The
Winner's
Edge

The Winner's Edge

Arthur Bruce Irwin

Collins Toronto

First published 1983
by Collins Publishers
100 Lesmill Road, Don Mills, Ontario

© 1983 Arthur Bruce Irwin

Canadian Cataloguing in Publication Data
   Irwin, Arthur Bruce, 1929-
     The winner's edge

   ISBN 0-00-217104-X

   1. Gambling systems   2. Irwin, Arthur Bruce, 1929-
   3. Gamblers — Biography.   I. Title.

   GV1302.I7   795'.01   C83-098315-5

Printed and bound in Canada
by John Deyell Company

Foreword

For a brief period more than twenty years ago, when I came out of the army, I made my living as a professional gambler in Europe. Therefore, when we, as a company, were approached by Bruce Irwin who had written a book explaining his system for consistently winning at casino gambling, I was most sceptical.

However, there was no way that Bruce, with his charm and persistence, would let us reject the book until he had proven that the system works. This he did at an editorial meeting about a week later. In the stunned silence that followed, it seemed that most people were dreaming of huge profits made in the casinos. Two sceptics remained, myself and my Executive Vice-President, Morton Mint.

In order to be convinced that the system really worked, we agreed to attend Bruce Irwin's gambling school and then visit a casino to test the system under field conditions.

Mort and I spent three long evenings being instructed by Bruce. It felt more like hard work than gambling, but by the third evening our mistakes had been ironed out and we understood the system.

The big day came early one Sunday morning when we flew on a gamblers' junket to the Playboy Club in Atlantic City. We each had $1,000 to play with. The flight on the Worldways Convair 640 was uneventful, but on arrival in Atlantic City we were met by a bus crewed with "bunnies." The pace was picking up! The biggest surprise was the casino itself. There were rooms the size of football fields built on top of one another, each one filled with roulette, blackjack, craps, and baccarat tables, and surrounded by one-armed bandits. There was hardly room to move with so many people playing — and this was at 10:30 A.M.!

Only having a small "roll" by professional gambling standards, I settled down at a roulette wheel with the target of winning $20 at a time. In Bruce's terminology, to win that targeted amount is to complete one sequence. The wheel did not seem to be with me. Just playing red and black I lost eleven, then nine times in a row, but each time I stuck to the system and won the $20. On one sequence I was down $400, but by playing the system I came out, in three spins of the wheel, $20 ahead.

At the end of the day, when it was time to catch the bus back to the airport, I counted my winnings. After deducting all expenses I had won $330 — not bad for one day's work. And it *was* work, because total concentration was needed.

Mort started off playing roulette, but then, still using the system, switched to blackjack. Altogether he won two more $20 sequences than I did.

Bruce kept a fatherly eye on us from a distance and, when we were not playing, did a little gambling. I saw him win $2,300 in three minutes playing blackjack.

The system had proved itself, and Bruce's claims were justified. To ensure that this first trial was not a fluke, another casino visit was made with similar results!

The system is not for everyone. A high degree of discipline and concentration is needed to make it work. It's not always fun, and it's hard work, but for those of you who want to play at the casino tables, the system explained in these pages can give you the "winner's edge."

Nick Harris,
President,
Collins Publishers

Contents

Foreword   5

Introduction   9

CHAPTER 1
Banks all over the world   13

CHAPTER 2
Roller skates, craps and ruin   15

CHAPTER 3
Death brings Lady Luck to heel   25

CHAPTER 4
You can beat the machine but
not the mechanic   31

CHAPTER 5
Canadian newsmen are
from Missouri   40

CHAPTER 6
Most casinos don't
lose — some won't   45

CHAPTER 7
A breath of honesty   53

CHAPTER 8
Half a bankroll is worse
than none   58

CHAPTER 9
I had overstayed my welcome   63

CHAPTER 10
Europe — Where the green
felt's greener   66

CHAPTER 11
New problems in the Old World   69

CHAPTER 12
The supreme test   76

CHAPTER 13
Case histories   82

CHAPTER 14
My test aboard the Hudson   95

CHAPTER 15
My introduction into
show business   98

CHAPTER 16
Our first trip together   104

CHAPTER 17
Married new year's eve
and a three and a half month
honeymoon   106

CHAPTER 18
School for gamblers   115

CHAPTER 19
Getting around in London   119

CHAPTER 20
Barred in England   **123**

CHAPTER 21
Interesting escapades   **135**

CHAPTER 22
Barred in Atlantic City   **140**

CHAPTER 23
Junkets   **146**

CHAPTER 24
Birth of Las Vegas of the North   **155**

CHAPTER 25
Introducing a new form
of entertainment   **163**

CHAPTER 26
Pilot project in
licenced premises   **167**

CHAPTER 27
The rules for riches:
memory, not magic   **174**

APPENDIX
How to play the games   **177**

The secret of success   **189**

Introduction

This book explains the secrets of my unbeatable system for winning at casino gambling — a system which I have used successfully at all gambling games in which even, given odds are offered. Since this system has proven its ability to win *all the time*, under every possible test — even matched against an electronic computer — it would seem expedient to simply publish the formula with easy-to-follow instructions and bid the reader good luck. But as this system wins money for one person from another, it is necessary for you to know how to create the right mental attitude that is required to use the system most successfully.

In almost every case my system will be used for profit in a gambling casino — and casinos are big business. Like any other business venture their aim is to win — to make a profit — and their whole operation is designed to make sure they win most of the time.

While most legalized casinos throughout the world are rigidly policed against cheating, it does, unfortunately, go on. Naturally, there is a big risk involved for the casinos, but their goal is money and some will do anything for money.

Thus, if the reader plans to use my system to make a profit for himself, it must be realized that inside or outside the casino, three human weaknesses — greed, pride and lack of discipline — are always at work. Acceptance of this fact will go a long way in preventing you from sallying forth like a lamb to the slaughter.

Cheating is no stranger to many Nevada casinos.

Legalized casinos are policed by various bodies,

depending on the country, such as special police squads, government departments or gambling commissions. While these groups are, in the main, scrupulously honest and dedicated to their task of keeping casinos free from cheaters, it is impossible for their officers or inspectors to be at every table all the time. Perhaps the most dedicated of these bodies is the Nevada Gaming Control Board which, through its untiring efforts, is mainly responsible for the popularity that state enjoys with gamblers and tourists. But even under the eagle-eyed scrutiny of the NGCB, cheating is no stranger to many Nevada casinos.

Cheating usually takes place in casinos — and I have visited these gambling centers in many parts of the world — when a patron is a big or consistent winner. Possession of the system contained in this book equips anyone to be one or the other — or both.

I know from experience that if gambling was all that I did, traveling all over the world and playing in the casinos, eventually I would reach a saturation point — or all the casinos would bar me from playing. I have never used the casinos for my sole livelihood, not only because I want something more from life, but because I know what happens behind the scenes; pit-bosses on the telephone, two or three of them standing over your shoulder watching you, snide remarks muttered about you — anything to upset you.

There is no doubt in my mind that I can walk into a casino at any time and make money.

I anticipate the expected and the unexpected every time I walk into a casino. Yet while it is of no interest to me to make the system my way of life, when the chips are down and I need money and I have the bankroll, there is no doubt in my mind that I can walk into any casino at any time and make money — any amount of money, in proportion to the bankroll that I am carrying.

I have endeavored to prepare this book in a way that not only allows the reader to master this unbeatable system, but also to profit from some of my experiences on active duty in casino combat. The old saying "a fool and his money are soon parted" is especially true of a person unprepared for the green-felt arena.

Arthur Bruce Irwin

CHAPTER 1

Bank accounts all over the world

I am probably one of the most fortunate people alive today—I have bank accounts all over the world. But my banks are casinos. For me, a casino is just like a bank—it just takes me a little longer to make a withdrawal. As long as I have some money to start playing, I can go into any casino in the world and make money.

When my business suffered a loss of over $100,000 in the 1970's I took half a dozen trips to the Caribbean. Within three months I had recovered my losses, paid all my debts and was again able to launch some new and profitable business ventures.

Gambling does not excite me anymore. The only reason that I gamble in casinos is because I always win money. Frankly, I don't love playing cards, and there is no casino game that thrills me.

The only reason that I gamble in casinos is because I always win.

I've spent so many years in the gambling business that I am aware of all the goings-on that take place behind the scenes. The glamor has long since vanished. Gambling is not my profession—it is the way I earn extra money. I've studied gambling for twenty-two years, trained at it and go about my gambling business in a professional manner. Gambling to me is a very shrewd, cold, calculating business. But a business it is, so far as I am concerned; for me, it holds none of the excitement that it does for the average person going to Las Vegas, Atlantic City or the Caribbean. For me it's a means of making money. Nothing more, nothing less.

I always set a limit of how much I want to win, and once I have met my objective, I walk away from the table. No addiction here. I can visit a casino resort for a week and go into the casino just one or two nights. My expenses for the entire holiday are covered plus I've made a profit, and that's it. Back to the sunshine. It's not my style to open and close the casino. In some cases, I'm in and out in no more than twenty minutes' time. Gambling, you see, is a business. Not a holiday, not an addiction, not an adventure. It's the way I earn money playing like a machine and eliminating emotion and human weakness. What sets my job apart from most is that I can make as much money as I want, whenever I choose. The secret of my success is in this book.

CHAPTER 2

Roller skates, craps and ruin

Frozen exhaust fumes reflected the bloody glare of the flashers back at the fire trucks as they blocked the street in front of the tall apartment building.

It was in Toronto, crackling from the first taste of winter, the fire season. There was smoke inside the building, and things were happening. Firemen were running in, and people were running out, coats pulled hastily over their pajamas. Some people carried young children, others held whatever prized possession they could grab when the alarm rang. An old man carried a photo album. A little old lady had an armload of china figurines. A rumpled blonde clutched a mink stole. But I, dressed in striped pajamas and a robe, had a little black book in one hand and a roulette wheel in the other.

"Now there's a gambler"

A fireman, stumbling under the weight of a hose, grinned back at his mate. "Now there's a gambler," he said.

Wrong. I hadn't gambled in some time. I'd played a lot, but it was no gamble. The dog-eared little black book took care of that.

I'd had my jousts with Lady Luck, like

everyone else. And perhaps I would never have grabbed the weapon that was to hold her at bay if she hadn't given me a terrible beating on her favorite playground — Las Vegas. That was back in 1951. In those days, I was bent on burning my name in history with a pair of roller skates. I was pretty good, and I had elected to leave Toronto to take on the top champs at the Hollywood Rollerdome, in California.

The westbound flight included a four-hour stopover in Las Vegas. The four hours were to stretch to fifty hours. They were to be among the longest, most costly, as well as the most educational, hours of my life.

I had breezed off the plane, thinking to myself something about when in Rome — or Las Vegas — go native. Why not, I mused, do a little gambling. There was $700 in my wallet — I could afford a little flutter.

There's a kind of electricity just short of hysteria in the room and it grabs you as soon as you're in the door.

I'd seen casinos in the movies and figured I knew what to expect. This error was the first in a shattering series of shocks.

Stepping off the street into a casino is something like falling out of bed into a cement mixer. If you survive, you never forget it.

The atmosphere of the casino hits all five senses at once. It's hearing, seeing, smelling, feeling and tasting. There's a kind of electricity just short of hysteria in the room and it grabs you as soon as you're in the door.

I think the first thing I noticed was the

people. Hundreds of them, staring hypnotized at the slot machines they were tugging, coaxing, wrenching. There was a strange, fierce detachment about them as they battled the one-armed bandits. Over the strains of popular music blasting from loud speakers, and the relentless whirr from the machines' steel guts, I could hear them. They crooned to the machines. They cursed them. They cajoled them.

Vaguely, I became aware of different people moving among the machines. Change girls. They flitted through the ranks of gamblers, responding with a businesslike smile to the ring of a jackpot bell, or the call for more nickels, dimes, quarters, half dollars or silver dollars to feed the mechanical beasts.

But this was just my first impression. Forcing down the excitement inside me, I pushed cautiously ahead. The noises were still there— but they were different noises. Along with the slot machines, there were people playing craps, blackjack and roulette. Here was the real magic of the casino. Just people, cards, dice and a free-spinning wheel. And Dame Fortune. I couldn't see her but I could feel her presence.

The odds sound great, but in the gambling jungle it's called a Sucker Bet.

I wandered from table to table, fascinated, then slipped over to the bar where I could study the whole scene through a martini glass.

The action at the crap table finally got me. I never saw a $20 bill vanish so fast. I decided to bet the twenty on the "field." This means that if any of the numbers 2, 3, 4, 9, 10, 11 or 12 come up, you win. The odds sound great, but in the gambling jungle it's called a sucker bet. There are all these chances to win — but dice just naturally produce more sixes, sevens and eights than any other numbers. There are more combinations of spots on the dice to produce these numbers than any of the field numbers.

I didn't know this. And when the hollow feeling had left the pit of my stomach, I decided that I hadn't really expected to win on my first bet anyway — and plunged on blindly to the slaughter. Forty bucks on the field. Seven came up on the dice. Eighty dollars on the field. Another seven on the dice.

A truism about gamblers is that they make their first bet for fun — and the rest to win back what they've lost. I was not only a gambler, but a wet-behind-the-ears outsider, caught up by the casino fever.

It was obvious that one of the field numbers had to come up soon — so I bet $160. This time the dice said five.

The rest of the world had gone by this time. Through a hot haze all I could see was the dice, the bored look on the pit-boss' face — and $320 I was betting on the field. Five again.

I'd lost $700 in less than five minutes.

Panic-stricken and angry, I threw my last $80 down. The dice rolled to a stop. Four on one, three on the other.

I remember hearing a yell of delight. It seemed to come from a long way off, but must have been from someone at the table. Someone with money on seven.

My mouth was dry. There was a pound of clay wedged in my throat. I wanted to throw up.

I staggered from the table like a drunk. The unbelievable truth kept hammering through my head. I'd lost $700 in less than five minutes.

I left the casino, like a drowning man fighting for the surface. I just wanted to be out of there, to breathe fresh air.

I stood in the street. I had sixty-five cents in my pocket, and a return ticket to Toronto. That ticket was my only hope.

Sorry, the clerk said, no refund on the ticket. It could only be cashed where it was bought. I caught the look the clerk gave his assistant. Yonder, it said, goes another sucker.

I had to agree. Never again. Never in a million years.

I found a phone booth, and called Toronto collect. I managed to arrange for $150 to be wired to me the next day.

There's nothing like a good night's sleep to cure the ills of the soul, and I awoke refreshed. The $150 had arrived, and I decided to walk around town to kill time until the next flight for Hollywood.

In twenty minutes I was in another casino.

I don't know why. The horror of last night was somehow pushed to the back of my mind. The money in my pocket and the leering, taunting front of the casino just made me want to get back in the fight. I'd get my money back.

I pushed past the crowded craps table, pretending it wasn't there, and studied the action at the blackjack setup. It looked simple, and I had a fair idea of the rules of the game.

Soon, I was in the game. And soon, I was winning. Confidence returned like a long-lost friend, and within twenty minutes I was twenty bucks ahead.

This, I told myself, is my game. The way I

was playing, I could win. So I started increasing the bets.

I'd grabbed the bait like a hungry bass, and the hook was set in minutes. Within an hour I was down to $10, and the intense nausea of yesterday returned. I kept fighting back the sickening realization that I had now lost $840 in two quick tries for easy money. I went out to clear the smell of the casino from my system.

You probably need to eat a lot more than I need to be stuck with another watch.

On the street, I thought it out. There was no hope of raising more money anywhere. I'd been forty-eleven kinds of a fool. All that remained was to take my licking like a man, and make the best of a desperate situation.

Oddly, this thought helped.

I knew that I wanted out of Las Vegas.

A watch that would fetch $25 in a pawnshop anywhere else got me a dollar and a half. The philosopher behind the counter, heavy on advice and short on sympathy, put it this way: "Look, son. I could give you more for this watch. But if I do, you'll sure as hell gamble it away. If I give you a buck and a half, you'll use the money to eat. You probably need to eat a lot more than I need to be stuck with another watch."

Maybe he was right. He'd seen a lot of guys like me.

I wandered into a restaurant and ordered a coffee and sandwich. It was a strange experience, drinking that coffee. I wanted to make it last forever — sipping it carefully, acutely aware that it had taken a significant chunk of all the money I had.

Over the rim of the cup, I noticed a large

well-dressed man sitting next to me. He was sizing me up like a farmer assessing a sickly steer. I managed a weak smile, and he grinned back.

"Tables get you?" he asked—like you'd ask a drippy-nosed, red-eyed character if he had a cold.

"Yes." Then I poured out the whole story. The sympathetic ear did me so much good that I blew another dime on a coffee for this big, good-natured guy. Big Jim.

He told me his story. He was from Arkansas, and he loved to gamble. Every so often he'd come to Vegas and on this trip he'd started with five grand. In five days he'd built his stake to $12,000. Then he lost it, all in one night.

But he didn't seem to care. In fact, he said he felt lucky.

"What y'got left?" he asked. I hauled out $1.85.

"You want to win your money back?"

I looked at the money again. I saw a few sandwiches and a few coffees in my hand. He picked up the dollar bill.

"Let me give it a try," he said.

"What in the world can you do with a dollar?" I asked.

"I feel lucky, I told you," said Jim. "Let's go."

Some of his carefree optimism had rubbed off on me — so we went.

We entered the Keno parlor of the big casino. Keno is something like Bingo. You buy a card marked with eighty numbers. On the cheapest card you mark two numbers. If they're called—you win. For more money, you can buy five, ten, up to fifteen number cards. Depending on the number of digits you've checked off that are called — you can win up to $25,000. The numbers called are flashed on a huge board — just like Bingo.

If you're going to gamble, you've got to believe you're going to win.

It takes five minutes to run off a Keno game. A shapely blonde in a green uniform and a seductive smile brought our cards. Jim selected a thirty-five cent bet, and marked nine numbers. He weighed the card in his hand, like someone trying to decide how much postage to put on a package.

"Getting any vibrations?" I asked, because it seemed like the intelligent thing to say at the time.

"Yes," said Big Jim.

I guess I must have looked sort of hard at him, because he said, "I know that sounds crazy, but I really do. I've an uncanny feeling of luck. We could hit with this card."

"Never knock your luck," Jim said. "If you're going to gamble, you've got to believe you're going to win."

This wasn't easy for me after the last two days of bad luck.

The game was starting. The ping-pong balls were bubbling around in their little glass box like one of those television jackpot shows. The first ball spat out, and the number flashed on the board. It wasn't one of our numbers.

The machine ejected more little balls — and Jim stared like a hungry tiger at the board. He was trying to will the right numbers to light up.

The last number flashed on the board, and Jim sighed. "Well, pal, that's too bad." I gave him a concerned look I'd been using a lot lately.

"Oh, we won," he said, "but not as much as I thought we would." He had five numbers right. Five bucks.

I had just about formed the thought: "How much help is $5?" when I noticed Jim's exhilaration.

"Let's have a celebration drink," he roared, and ordered two shots of rye. I needed the drink, but it hurt to watch our newfound wealth shrink by $2. I thought of claiming my share and quitting—but the spirit of Big Jim and Mr. Seagram kept me in my chair.

Jim took the new card from the girl, shut his eyes and flared his nostrils. "Not this one," he said. "It's dead." His good-natured mysticism was starting to get to me too. The next card, he said, felt better. Again, he was right.

"I think we've done a little better this time," he grinned. Right again. He picked eight numbers. Twelve hundred dollars! I'd forgotten there was that kind of money.

"Believe in my luck now?" he said. I couldn't answer. I was fanning those incredible bills and laughing like a four-year-old at a cartoon matinee.

"Let's go," said Jim. I didn't answer; I just followed my savior like a pup!

I woke up when we arrived at his destination. The crap table in another casino. The same crap table that had turned me inside out. He bought $600 worth of chips and made nothing but side-bets.

I stood and watched, without really being aware of what was going on. I did notice that after a while he started to use a different color of chip — reaching back every now and again to hand me a black chip. I didn't know what they were worth, but after two hours I had a pocketful of them.

My legs were about to give out when Jim finally turned away and said, "Let's cash in. I can feel that feeling slipping away. You've got to believe in your luck."

There's only one way to describe the way I felt when we left the cashier's desk. Stoned. Higher than a kite. It had nothing to do with the rye.

It was the $1,500 — beautiful, crisp greenbacks — that I held in my hand.

I was babbling thanks at Jim. I'd never wanted to thank anyone so much before.

"Forget it," he said, in the same voice he used hours before — when he couldn't afford a coffee. "It was my luck — but your money."

Then he showed me his winnings. $26,000. I'd never seen that much money. Big Jim lifted my sagging jaw with his hand, and we headed for a bar.

We toasted luck. His luck. "You're like most people," he said. "You're not a gambler. You're the kind of guy the casinos depend on for their profits. You'll have little wins — but you'll lose in the long haul. No offence, buddy — that's the way it is. Me — I'm a gambler. It's in my system and I have a feeling for it. I give it two months in the year because I have to. You don't have to; so if you want to gamble, take a little flutter. Don't play big. You'll save yourself a lot of heartache."

I hung on every word of the sermon, which was delivered over the lip of a whisky glass. And I promised Big Jim I would follow his advice. And I have. I never gambled again, although I've taken thousands of dollars out of casinos since Jim wiped his mouth, shook my hand and walked into the hot Las Vegas night.

CHAPTER 3

Death brings Lady Luck to heel

I've never been able to shake the idea that tele-grams bring bad news. So my mood matched the drizzly Vancouver weather when the boy handed me the envelope.

The news was bad, all right. My Uncle Murray, a favorite uncle, was in hospital in Toronto. He probably wasn't going to make it, and he was asking for me. I liked old Murray and was eager to be with him.

Be content with a few dollars a day.

In the antiseptic gloom of the hospital room, it was evident that the end was close. The old man knew it too, and told me I was to have some-thing he had kept to himself all his life. But I had to promise it would never be used in a way that would hurt anyone.

The faint, familiar voice told me that I was to get his mathematical system for gambling — a system that would win at any game where the odds are even. He had to fight for each breath as he explained it. And he kept saying, "Use your head, son. Be content with a few dollars a day."

After the funeral, I received a sealed enve-lope. I went back to Vancouver to nurse a small business I was trying to get off the ground. Although I had an opportunity to open and read the letter explaining the system, it was a good month before I had the chance to put the system into effect with the small roulette wheel I had purchased.

Uncle Murray's system was spelled out clinically, like a chemical formula. I knew he had been a whiz at mathematics, but I had never heard of him gambling. I was amused, but my strongest reaction was skepticism. I'd heard about gambling systems. Everyone has. And anyone with a brain knows they can't work.

But with this was the nagging knowledge that the old man was no joker and no fool. He was a man who had lived alone most of his life, preferring his books to people. If it wasn't a joke, I reasoned, and if it really worked, it would be like having the key to Fort Knox. But the idea of a winning system was too far-fetched. The system went into a desk drawer to be forgotten until a rainy Sunday afternoon a month later.

I took the system from its drawer and read it again. Then I got a deck of cards and dealt myself a few hands of blackjack, following the system with my bets.

I won. I continued to play, and continued to win. By this time I was really excited. It was late, and I put away the cards and went to bed — but not to sleep.

My head was cluttered up with the mathematics involved in the system—but one simple equation kept pounding through my brain: three hundred hands of blackjack, plus uncle's system, had equalled winning hundreds of dollars on paper.

Despite every test, the system continued to win.

I got up next morning, weary but determined. I drove down the rain-slick streets and shopped for every book I could find on gambling. I was going to test this system every way I knew how.

For three weeks, every spare minute was spent attacking the system. I tested it with every game I could find. I racked my brain to find a chink in the mathematical armour, to prove the system could fail.

Despite every test, the system continued to win. The tests were all made on paper. I decided that the real test would be a game where I played for real money. Maybe this would show a flaw.

The Pacific National Exhibition was on in Vancouver at the time and there was a game of chance there. I took a hundred dollars and went to the fair.

The game was called Under Seven or Over Seven. On the spin of a wheel, the bettor can put his money on over or under for even money or on seven for odds of three-to-one. The operator, or maybe the law, had put a $5 limit on the bets, and the odds were even. I decided on a twenty-five cent first bet.

I played for about three hours, and although I won very little money, I won steadily. The system was proving itself but I still wasn't satisfied.

I went back next day, and ranged my bets from ten cents to $3.

The operator recognized me from the previous day. After watching me for a while, he sneered, "You must have a system, Mac." I confessed, and he laughed out loud. "Another sucker."

He stopped laughing after a while. He even started to frown a lot. The system continued to win.

I came back again the next day. I'd been playing about half an hour when a midway official took me aside. He didn't know what I was doing, he confessed, nor did he know how I was doing it. He did know, however, that the game concession was supposed to make money, and that I was preventing this. I could play as long as I liked — but I was now limited to fifty-cent bets.

This made it difficult to play the system, so I quit.

I quit happy. In three days I'd played about five hours with an original stake of $100. I had a profit of $47.25.

There was just one more test that I could throw at the system — combat conditions in the big league. I drew $800 out of the bank and, accompanied by a friend, booked a flight to Las Vegas for the acid test.

I checked into the Flamingo Hotel, then gave the system a final check on my tiny roulette wheel before stepping into the blistering desert air and heading for a casino.

I strutted into the nearest casino with a confidence I'd never had on previous trips, and changed $10 into chips.

Some of the old nervousness came back when I approached the roulette wheel — but after half an hour's play with ten-cent chips, I was ahead the exact amount I had aimed for. I switched to twenty-five cent chips, and my confidence grew with my winnings. My only problem was fighting back the urge to make really big bets.

I switched to fifty-cent chips, and fifteen minutes later I had made my goal again. By the time I left, I had won $175.

The casino officials were taking good hard looks at me.

I slept well that night, in the crisp air-conditioning of the hotel. Next day it was a hundred and two in the shade at noon, but I hardly noticed as I waltzed to the nearest casino. I played for four hours and won $600.

It was different this time, though. I was no longer a face in the crowd. The casino officials were taking a good hard look at me.

I thought nothing of it at the time, although later I was to learn some of the unpleasant things that can happen to a consistent winner.

I was evening the score with the casinos and I was happy.

After dinner I played some more. I had cashed in, and was counting my $1,200 winnings when a pit-boss cornered me. He handed me two free tickets to the casino's stage show. I'd barely recovered from this sudden display of generosity, when he invited me to move out of the Flamingo and into a room at his casino — free.

This one I questioned. Part of their public relations policy, he said. I'd been doing most of my gambling at this place, and the casino liked to keep its customers.

Even as a greenhorn I translated this to read, "You've won more than $2,000 here. We want you around to win it back."

Confident that the invitation couldn't have the desired effect, I accepted.

As show time was three hours away, I continued to play and continued to win.

For the next couple of days I was the center of attention. Wherever I went—from table to table, and from casino to casino—as soon as I took out my little black book to calculate bets, there was a lot of muttering among pit-bosses, wheelmen and dealers. The cards were changed often. So were the dealers.

Sometimes they'd change dealers five times in fifteen minutes.

It didn't rattle me. I decided—and long-time casino habitués have since borne my theory out—that the switching of dealers, the breaking out of new cards, is part of the psychological war the casino wages on consistent winners.

With my formula, however, none of these moves can affect the outcome as long as the player keeps his head. The only way the house can beat you is by introducing a "mechanic."

This guy doesn't fix cars. It's the name they give a highly skilled shark, an expert cheater. Against these lovelies—no system can work.

CHAPTER 4

You can beat the machine but not the mechanic

The system was a weapon that could set me up for life — but it didn't take me long to realize that I needed a bankroll. No problem. Anyone, I reasoned, would be happy to provide a bankroll to get my foolproof passport to riches off the ground. There would be a quick, substantial return on the investment.

Another mistake. Everyone I demonstrated the system to was impressed — but not sufficiently impressed to put up the money. The ones who showed the most interest either wanted to know the system — or wanted most of the winnings. The others treated the whole thing like an amusing parlor game.

These are the kind of people who could find the map to Captain Kidd's treasure, frame it, and hang it in the recreation room between the crying towels.

It was late summer, and I was starting to really worry about where the bankroll was going to come from, when it occurred to me that this was the silly season in the newspaper world. The season when there's very little hard news, and the papers fight with each other to dig up oddball stories.

I'll give them a story, I thought, if they'll loan me some money.

A phone call brought a well-dressed reporter with an analytical eye to my apartment. I'd been talking to him for about fifteen minutes when he decided that I needed a psychiatrist more than a journalist. His incisive questions dwindled as I talked. Soon, he was reduced to making polite noises, and clearing his throat a lot. His eyes kept wandering to the door, like a caged animal weighing his chances of escape.

The newspapers would advance me $5,000, and I'd take a reporter to Las Vegas for a week.

The only way to keep him was a demonstration. I hauled out the wheel, and told him to bet how and where he liked. All I told him was the amount to bet on each spin.

In half an hour he'd changed his mind about me. He'd won, on paper, about a month's salary. I gave him the proposition: the newspapers would advance me $5,000, and I'd take a reporter to Las Vegas for a week. At the end of the week I'd return the bankroll and the paper could run a series on the system at work under combat conditions. I'd keep the profit after expenses.

But the hard-bitten editors were from Missouri. Their first reaction was that some idiot was trying to take them for $5,000 with a minimum of effort.

So I had to show them.

In most newspaper offices there's a game going somewhere. Normally it's in the dark room, where off-duty photographers indulge in some clandestine poker.

But the scene in the city room the next day was something else. Reporters and editors huddled round a rattling roulette wheel slap in the middle of the rewrite desk. They saw, they made bets and they won. But they weren't convinced.

Later at the Press Club, someone mentioned a chess-playing computer. IBM, he said, had a computer programmed to play blackjack.

There was a hint of a sneer in the voice that asked me if I'd be prepared to stack my system up against the machine. I accepted without hesitation.

October 15, 1962 was the date of the strangest gambling session Toronto has ever seen. Inside the IBM center, I eyed the opposition. There were two photographers, a couple of reporters, three mathematicians, a smattering of technicians — and the machine.

1620 was the name of my opponent. I sat down at a small desk, with a tiny control panel. To my right was an electric typewriter. To my left, a machine that looked like a filing cabinet. It was IBM's card-shuffler. The cards were special punch-cards, perforated to represent a deck of cards.

The reporters told me how much they wanted me to win.

The machine evidently didn't trust me any more than the people from the fourth estate. It kicked off the game by snapping off a couple of questions on the typewriter.

Machine: Is it legal to gamble in California?

Me: (pecking with one finger) No.

Machine: How old are you?

Me: 32

This seemed to satisfy its circuits, because it printed out two headings:

PLAYER   DEALER

It started printing the cards being fed through its innards. Under Player it would print, say, 10C—ten of clubs. Under Dealer, 4H —four of hearts. And so on.

It was almost as dispassionate as a Las Vegas pit-boss.

The deal complete, it would ask if I wanted another card. If the answer was yes, I'd get another pair of digits.

The machine would then weigh the player's total against the dealer's total and print Dealer Wins or Player Wins, according to the outcome. It was almost as dispassionate as a Las Vegas pit-boss.

The machine played faster than any dealer I ever met, which meant that I had to work that much faster on my formula calculations. After five tests, I left that pile of machinery $796 richer, on paper, than I was when I came in.

I left the IBM center triumphant—only to have the steam let out of me the next day. The paper phoned to say that a big probe into gambling was underway in Ontario and for one of the big city dailies to underwrite a gambling experiment would be, to say the least, ill-timed.

They suggested, with the naivete papers sometimes show, that I reveal the system so that they could use it as a curb against gambling.

"Thanks," I said. "But no thanks."

I returned to British Columbia and during the course of a year or so I put on demonstrations for various clubs, but concentrated mainly on a course I was taking in dental work. On one occasion during that period I was persuaded by a friend to take a trip to Nevada. He would provide a $3,000 bankroll and we would split the profit equally. Before we left I explained, without disclosing the system, that the formula was geared to wins and losses. That how the bets were placed made no difference except for the fact that a run of losses would slow up the process of winning. Three or four wins would recoup what we had laid out and supply us with the amount we had set out to make on the particular sequence. We would then start again on another sequence. I emphasized the point that he would have to be prepared to see five, eight or ten or up to eighteen losses in a row if that was the way things went, but at no time would there be any reason for doubt or panic. He promised complete faith, almost pushing me into the car in his eagerness to get to the airport, to Reno, and to the bank.

After the first fifteen minutes in a Reno casino, we were $170 ahead. By the time we retired that night our profit stood at $400. My friend was almost ecstatic, but the weakness of human nature was to show through.

Next morning we went to another casino and I started playing roulette. Before an hour passed, I had pushed our profit to almost $700. Up until then I had experienced no more than three or four losses on any one sequence. Now, as sometimes happens, I had five losing bets in a row, then six, then ten, and finally fourteen.

As I have explained previously, all a series of losses amounts to is a slight annoyance, an extra ten or fifteen minutes to wait for the sequence to be completed and the desired amount won. But my friend began to panic. I reminded him of my warning that this could happen, but he brushed it aside demanding that I pull out now before any more money was lost.

At this point we were down about $500 — less than we had made. I left the table and took him to the bar where I tried to talk some confidence back into him. I was getting annoyed, but at the same time appreciated how a person felt when he saw his money disappearing. But regardless of what I said he could not bring himself to continue. Finally, my patience ran out. I handed him what chips I had left. He cashed in, and together with the bulk of the bankroll which I had insisted he keep, he left Reno.

As this trip was part of my vacation, I decided not to allow my friend's attitude to spoil it. I had brought some money of my own so I visited another casino, picked up the sequence where I had left off and after about ten minutes of play completed it successfully.

About six months later, needing a break from a period of intensive concentration, I again allowed myself to be persuaded to visit Nevada under similar conditions. But this time human nature produced a different twist. After the first day's playing we were about $500 ahead.

I decided to call it quits, have dinner and go to bed. My companion on this trip, who was carrying the $2,000 bankroll, which had grown to $2,200 with his share of the day's profit, said he would stroll around the city before turning in. The next morning I was greeted by a bleary-eyed, sad-looking figure. After leaving me the night before he had decided to "try a few hands" of blackjack. His few hands had developed into an all-night session in which he had gambled away every penny. Disgusted, I packed him into the car and headed for the airport and back to Vancouver.

During the time that followed I had many more offers from people who wanted to back me, but I refused them all. I had no intention of risking the chance of a repeat performance. Solo travel with a modest bankroll seemed a better idea.

I didn't play big because I didn't need to win big.

A trip to Nevada would be a holiday with an unlimited bank account. At my casino bank it just took a little longer to make a withdrawal.

I didn't play big because I didn't need to win big. Just $20 from this casino, $30 from that one. Because I moved around a lot and didn't make big wins, I went unnoticed, and was on friendly terms with the staff of most of the clubs in town.

I was to learn later how casinos react to big, consistent winners.

One evening, during a stay in Reno, I had made arrangements to meet one of my friends at a casino in Sparks, which is only a stone's throw from Reno proper.

As I entered the club I found my friend sitting at a blackjack table, killing time just betting a few dollars on each hand. Approaching the table I could see four empty seats, so I proceeded to sit in, and bought $500 worth of chips.

Standing across from me was a sweet little old gray-haired lady.

After having played a dozen hands (on my luck) and losing, I pulled out my little black book and started to use my system. After two or three hands the dealer was changed, and now standing across from me was a sweet little old gray-haired lady, whom I might add was a new face to me in this casino. Without knowing what was about to happen I continued to play, and continued to lose. Having lost my $500 I moved to the next table and cashed another $500. Within a couple of hands this dealer was changed and again the little old lady was shuffling the cards for the next hand.

It only took her twenty-five minutes to win my $500. She never made any conversation during our game. And the cards appeared to be coming faster and faster.

Leaving this table I moved to the one on my right, cashed another $500 and immediately the dealer was replaced by my gray-haired friend, winning all my money before I had the chance to smoke a couple of cigarettes.

Up to now I had lost $1,500, so moving to yet another table, I cashed $700, only to find her standing in front of me again before I had even the opportunity to warm the seat.

After losing another three hands, I asked her if she was following me from table to table. She replied, "No, the shift is changing and you're moving from table to table in the same order."

I had no reason to disbelieve her, yet I was becoming astonished at the number of losses, and as they continued to mount it was only a short while before my $700 had disappeared.

Realizing I had dropped $2,200, I left the table to recalculate my mathematics, only to see this sweet old lady hand the deck of cards she had been using to the pit-boss, who placed them in his desk. He then handed her a sweater from the back of a chair, which she placed around her shoulders and left the casino.

At the bar my friend and I took stock. Out of 147 hands, I had lost 123, tied 9 and won 15.

It was not until some eight months later, after reading Professor Thorp's book, *Beat the Dealer*, that this sweet-looking little old lady was revealed to me. She was the same one Thorp had encountered during his less successful travels throughout Nevada.

That was my first experience of being "mechaniced." By the way, I carried on the next day and recouped my losses at another casino.

CHAPTER 5

Canadian newsmen are from Missouri

Doug, a friend of mine, ran the best pizza-palace in Scarborough—a Toronto suburb not renowned for its beaneries. I was watching Doug over a slab of Parmesan and mushroom when he walked up to me, another guy in tow.

He introduced me to Ron Dunn, a reporter for the *Toronto Telegram*. Ron was interested to hear I'd just returned from Reno—and the conversation quite naturally drifted to gambling and systems. Ron, it seems, knew a man with a system that worked at the race track. He lived off it, and quite handsomely.

When he told the yarn I felt a warm glow. Here was someone I could tell about my system, without getting that familiar look—half pity, half smile.

He was interested. But when I told him my system never failed, his eyes glazed somewhat. I trotted out a coin, which I proceeded to flip.

I told him how to bet, and within an hour he had "won" $200. Now he was listening very carefully to everything I had to say.

He wasn't idle for the next twenty-four hours. By the time I met him for a drink the following afternoon, he'd checked me out fairly thoroughly—including the IBM story.

He rounded up a couple of his friends and devised a new test for the system. While the trio sat in an apartment spinning a roulette wheel — I was in a phone booth across the street, getting reports on their wins and losses and telling them how to bet accordingly. The system, of course, came through with flying colors, and Ron was now a believer.

He was sure his paper would be interested in the story — and I offered the *Telegram* the same deal as I had offered the *Star*. And I got the same response. Fine, but not with our money.

Ron was more disappointed by the management decision than I was. I'd become hardened to skepticism. Then one day a couple of weeks later, he introduced me to Bruce Baxter. I should have met this man years before. The meeting changed the course of my life.

Bruce was the kind of man you see in cigarette and beer commercials — you know the kind, big in build and big in outlook, knows what he likes and goes after it with both hands.

I demonstrated my method. At first he was wary and didn't say much, but after a return visit to Ron's apartment and another demonstration he declared that he was convinced it worked as I claimed and made reservations for a flight to Las Vegas.

He was putting up a $5,000 bankroll, and Ron's managing editor, Andy MacFarlane, had given Ron the OK for the expenses-paid trip.

I felt almost smug as I leaned back in my seat, staring dreamily at the "fasten your seat belts" sign. At last, I was on my way.

The neon lights of Las Vegas looked like a bed of roses to me as the big jet nosed down on Lady Luck's home town. As Bruce, Ron and I walked down the ramp, the stewardess gave us the regulation airline smile, and the farewell they reserve for this airfield only: "Good Luck."

We'd gained three hours in our flight west,

and we stepped into the hot Nevada air a little after 9 PM. Vegas would hardly have come to life for the night.

We walked out the echoing tunnel from the terminal past the inevitable row of slot machines.

I'm convinced that the Nevada Coat of Arms should be a pair of one-armed bandits, rampant, on a field of all-day suckers.

The Stardust has a gimmick that brings out the kid in people.

We decided to stay at the Stardust, and as the hot breath of the Las Vegas night came at us through the cab's open window, we were already gripped by the magic of the place. The seductive neon of the Strip flickered over our faces.

The cabbie filled us in with all sorts of trivia about the gambling capital. He pointed out an ominously dark building. An elaborate casino that never opened.

The State of Nevada polices its casinos pretty strictly and, according to our chauffeur, the Gambling Control Board wasn't satisfied with a number of the proposed board of directors of the new casino — so it didn't open.

The Stardust has a gimmick that brings out the kid in people. They drive you to your room in a little white cart—something like a golf cart. The carts are practical as well as entertaining, because the huge accommodation wings spread out for hundreds of feet to either side of the main casino, like crossbars on a telephone pole.

Service in Las Vegas casinos and hotels is among the best in the world. Before we had time to change from our travel-weary business suits, a tray of cold drinks was in the room.

Bruce transferred his wallet from one pair of pants to another. He checked the contents. Five thousand dollars in traveller's checks, drawn on a Toronto bank. He'd bought the checks as a safety precaution against theft.

We got the kinks out of our legs by walking to a casino a few blocks away. Inside, Bruce changed $3,000 of traveller's checks into cash. I stuffed the bills into my pocket, walked over to the blackjack table, and turned the cash into chips.

The wheelman watched me carefully when I made the first calculation in my little black book.

I trotted out my little calculations book, licked the point of a pencil, and got ready to make my first bet.

"Not here." said the lugubrious pit-boss, his heavy black eyebrows punctuating the order. "You can't play a system at this table."

I tried arguing, but should have saved my breath. I moved to the roulette wheel. I played reds and blacks alternately.

The wheelman watched me carefully when I made the first calculation in my little black book. Then he seemed to ignore me completely.

From time to time, Bruce would wander over to see how I was doing, and murmur approval of the formula which was pulling me steadily ahead. I'd finished my first $50 sequence and was working on the next $50. I looked over my shoulder, and saw Bruce wrestling happily with the slot machines. I won the next three bets, which meant the sequence would be complete in record time.

The world, I decided, was a pretty good place. And Las Vegas was just a dandy place. And the casino was pure bliss.

But the casinos had an ace up their glittering sleeves — and they were to play it soon.

CHAPTER 6

Most casinos don't lose — some won't

We had become Las Vegas people already — which meant that rising before noon was unthinkable. Breakfast was brunch — and usually steak.

Bruce and I decided that we'd have a look at some of the lesser casinos in downtown Las Vegas. We were amazed at the activity in that section, even in the early afternoon.

The downtown casinos lack some of the opulence of the Strip — and they're a lot noisier, because they have more one-armed bandits. Noise means confusion, and confusion doesn't help a system player.

I bought $2,000 worth of chips and headed for the quietest roulette wheel. The young wheelman looked puzzled when I pulled out my calculating book — and nodded his head to the pit-boss, who was standing a few feet away. He held up the game several moments until a signal from the pit-boss gave him the green light to spin.

I took the precaution of asking the wheelman what the limit was on the game. This is always good policy — because if you don't know the limit, the result can be disastrous.

"Limit's two bits," he said, without looking my way.

"That's the minimum limit, isn't it?" I

asked. He didn't grace this one with an answer. But he looked with beseeching eyes at the pitboss, who didn't notice him. The wheelman, I decided, didn't know how to answer my last question.

I tried again, louder this time, "What's the maximum bet?"

He tried to look very busy paying off other patrons, and snapped over his shoulder, "Five hundred dollars."

Which was all I wanted to know.

I played twelve sequences of the system, and cleared $600. Big Bruce walked up, "How're we doing?"

"Fine," I said. "Getting weary of walking around?"

"Not at all," he said. "I'll feed some more nickels to the bandits."

A lot of people think that when a color hits three or four times in a row, the other color is due to connect.

He left, and I noticed I'd drawn a rooting section. Several people had gathered behind me as I played the wheel red, black, high, low — as the mood moved me.

There were gasps of amazement when I'd continue to play, say, black after it had hit four or five times. A lot of people think that when a color hits three or four times in a row, the other color is due to connect. This is the biggest single mistake you can make in roulette. I've seen the same color hit many, many times in a row.

Listening to them talk reminded me of an evening during one of my first visits to Las Vegas. I was playing at one of the larger clubs out on the Strip and, as I decided to play red all the time that particular evening, a man, dressed in a very smart business suit, stood behind me for more than an hour and watched intensely. At one point, when the red had hit four times in a row, he tapped me on the shoulder and said, "My God, son. Do you expect the red to win all the time?"

The odds are the same on each spin of the wheel, no matter what has happened before.

"No," I replied, "but my chances are more favorable by playing one color than by jumping back and forth as the black hits."

He stared down at me as though I was pulling his leg, and almost immediately a sheepish grin appeared, growing larger and larger as I continued to explain:

"The odds are the same on each spin of the wheel, no matter what has happened before. If I was to jump back and forth from one color to the other I could incur more losses, should the wheel start hitting red, black, red, black, red, black, than if I was to stand on the same color all the time."

With this he threw back his head and let out a hearty laugh, which now attracted some of the other onlookers. Half yelling and snorting, he stated, "You're sure a greenhorn, aren't you?"

I was becoming slightly embarrassed as the people were passing little remarks to each other in whispers. However, as I knew the system and he did not, I felt that I was playing it to the best of my ability. I shrugged off the feeling of resentment and continued to play, not forgetting his presence behind me as he continued to chatter with the other patrons as though he was an authority on the game.

After a dozen spins or so and still playing red all the time, the wheel began its frequent run of consistent colors, and red appeared five times in a row. One of the onlookers, bringing this to the attention of the man behind me, promptly pulled his wallet from his pocket as he pushed his way to the front and thrust a $50 bill on the black. Which he lost.

He placed another fifty, and lost, and by now he was getting a little worried as the people watching became quiet with eyes glued to the wheel for the next spin as he placed $100 on the black.

All bets down.

Even the wheelman, who previously had made his mechanical moves very nonchalantly, appeared aroused by the sudden interest of the players and the appearances of red hitting so many times in succession, which had now totalled nine wins.

"All bets down," he called, as the little white plastic ball bounced in and around the wheel. Suddenly, when all heads were bent forward, the spell was broken by a woman's voice exclaiming, almost hysterically, "Red won again."

By now it was apparent to see the pasty look on the man's face. He stared into the wheel, half hoping that a mistake had been made. Redness now started to show above his collar as he grabbed a handful of bills and thrust them down on the black, scattering the other chips played onto the floor.

As I had been playing a small sequence at the time, my bets were always lower than $50, due to the amount of wins I was having on the red. However, for the player of black, the bets were significant, and the strain was changing to anger. By now he had not only lost face with the people at the table, but had also lost a considerable amount of money. Looking around at the various faces at the table he pulled another $100 bill and, trying to force a grin, laid it on top of the $50 bill previously placed by him a few moments before.

By now, even the pit bosses had gathered to see what was causing the commotion. As they looked on, many of the people who had now gathered three deep around the table began placing bets — ranging from $5 to $500 — on the black. They were completely confident that for red to win again was an impossibility.

Slowly the ball lost its momentum, and settled into a black slot for a split second, before spinning out and resting in the red.

The commotion turned to near-bedlam. Many in the crowd left the table with heads down, some walked away still in shock, while new faces on learning what was happening, greedily rushed forward to change their cash into chips before the next spin.

For the next twenty-five minutes, thousands of dollars were bet and lost as red continued to win for a total of twenty-two consecutive spins.

Red had now won eleven times in a row. For the next twenty-five minutes, thousands of dollars were bet and lost as red continued to win for a total of twenty-two consecutive spins. On the twenty-third spin of the wheel black won, paying off a $25 bet, which had been placed by a gentleman who made some money on the red and had made this bet for the boys on the table.

I turned to see what had happened to the man who had stood behind me and learned that he had left the table, dejected and dumbfounded, having lost over $1,800 betting on the black.

To this day I still believe that there's a power responsible to prove, if nothing else, the fact that the impossible can happen.

On talking to the wheelman a short while later, he told me that in his thirty odd years of gaming, he had never seen a color hit so many consecutive times before. To this day, I still believe that there's a power responsible to prove, if nothing else, the fact that the impossible can happen.

It was the cocktail girl bringing me a drink that snapped me back to the present. I had a couple of drinks, then went back to work. I gradually increased our profit, when the wheel started going crazy again. After twenty minutes or so, I'd suffered far more losses than usual, and was betting in the neighborhood of $300 a spin.

This didn't bother me, because it had happened many times before and I knew I would regain my losses and make my target in time.

I was getting low on money, so I changed $1,000 for chips. I bet $426 on the black. The wheelman gave me just the hint of a doubtful look, took the bet — and black came up.

I had barely realized what happened, when the pit-boss came charging up like an aggravated rhinoceros, nearly knocking the wheelman into the aisle. Everyone fell back as though the joint was being raided. "No bet! No bet!" the pit-boss roared.

Astonished, I asked why.

"You're over the table limit," he said.

"Cool it," I said. "The limit's $500 and I only bet $426."

"Not a chance," he ranted. "The limit is $250."

I couldn't believe it. I explained that his very own wheelman had told me there was a $500 limit.

He was looking nervous, but kept his belligerent manner. "I set the limits here, not him."

Maybe your table limit depends on whether you're winning or losing?

I looked around. The other players were just as amazed as I was. The wheelman was studying the floor.

"Look pal," I said. "I've just had six or seven losses in a row from $250 to $326. There's four or five other people here who have lost on bets the same size. Maybe your table limit depends on whether you're winning or losing?"

I reminded him, hotly, that he had gotten the wheelman to cash the $1,000 so that I could increase my last bet from $326 to $426.

He just stood there, like a bully waiting for someone to take a swing. He had caught the eye of the casino guards — who looked as though they'd like nothing better than to see how much distance they could get out of me in a four-handed throw.

I picked up my remaining chips in disgust. I knew Vegas had thrown me another of the curves that come the way of a consistent winner.

Bruce and I went for a drink, and took stock. We'd dropped $2,500 at the roulette wheel — my first real loss since I learned the formula.

CHAPTER 7

A breath of honesty

There's this about Las Vegas. For every time you learn that some places are dishonest, you're given an example of the scrupulous honesty of other places.

Upon arriving at the Thunderbird Hotel on the Strip we decided to take a break from gambling. After handing all my remaining money to Bruce, we went to take in some of the shows, and somehow during the next three hours became separated.

After watching two or three lounge shows, I decided to see if Bruce was still around. Dropping back to the Thunderbird, the casino manager, to whom I had been introduced a day or two earlier, politely told me that Bruce was not around. After leaving a message that I had been by, I left to take in a movie down the street.

Finally, about four hours later, I returned to the club to find Bruce in the cocktail lounge enjoying another Las Vegas show. He began to tell me what had taken place earlier. It seemed that after we had become separated, he had returned to the club a few minutes after I had been asking about him. He apparently thought that as I had taken a slight break from gambling, I had returned to the club, expecting to find him there so that I could get the money and continue to play.

Even though Las Vegas is a gambling town, the casino management can be honest and beyond reproach.

Bruce, a little upset that he had missed me, walked over to the casino manager and explaining the circumstances, quite nonchalantly handed him $1,500 to give me if I should again come looking for him. During the next few hours, Bruce wandered about only to return and find that I had not come in again and was promptly handed the full $1,500 by the casino manager. All of which, I am sure, proves that even though Las Vegas is a gambling town some of the casino management are honest and beyond reproach. Ask yourself sincerely, would you walk up to a man whom you had met briefly a few days before and hand him $1,500 completely confident that the money was as safe as the Rock of Gibraltar? I am sure you would not.

This incident put a good taste back in my mouth—and we went back to the tables, where we recouped the losses incurred at the crooked casino downtown.

Bruce had to leave next day, to check on his business in Toronto. He left Ron and I to prove the system to Ron's city editor, Art Cole, who had decided to see the game for himself.

We met Art at the airfield, after a half-hour drive in the desert—the result of a wrong turn. But this man made the side trip worth while.

He's the result of three decades of dealing with people through the newspaper world. He's one of the most intelligent, well-informed people I've ever met. His company is delightful, his conversation sparkling and witty.

Yet he had the reputation of being a bear behind his city desk. Any newspaperman from

Toronto will tell you, when you've been chewed out by Art Cole, you've been chewed out by a man who makes a marine sergeant sound like a stuttering Sunday school teacher. But he'd never chewed a man out unless he was sure of his facts. That's what makes a good newspaperman, and for my money, that's what makes a good man.

We had a rest, a relaxed meal and headed back to the battlefield. I asked Art to pick his game — he chose blackjack.

Ten minutes later and $75 richer, we sauntered into the casino lounge.

"What do you think?" I asked.

He knit his brows, and leaned his chin on clasped hands. "It's impressive, Bruce, but. . . ."

I didn't expect him to be convinced on the first time out. Not this guy.

We went back, and parlayed $300 into $345 in five minutes. I took great care to let Art see the amount we started with, the amount of each bet, and let him count the chips when the sequence was complete.

The cynical newsman was starting to accept the fact that my formula was a winner.

We rounded the evening off with a show at the Stardust — and started the next evening with an extravagant meal and a show at the Desert Inn. I covered the cost of both evenings in a couple of hours of craps and roulette.

This sort of thing went on for the next four days. The only game I lost was golf. Art whipped the pants off both Ron and I on the links.

On the fourth evening, we all left for Toronto, with assurance that we would be in touch up there.

It was less than a week later that one of Art's men called me. All the top brass of the

Toronto Telegram wanted a demonstration of my system. As I wheeled my car onto the roof parking lot of the modern newspaper building overlooking Lake Ontario, I felt good.

The plush boardroom took on an atmosphere halfway between a courthouse and a casino. I had brought my roulette wheel, a deck of cards and a pair of dice.

Before me were arrayed some of the least gullible men in Canada. Andy MacFarlane — red-haired and sharp-witted. Doug McFarlane — a thoughtful man not inclined to take anyone's word for anything. Arnold Agnew, shrewd, analytic.

I followed my favourite pattern. I let them play — but I called the bets.

Several sequences later—the first question, and one I had anticipated. "If you can make $50 or $60 in a few minutes, why don't you stay at the tables for a few hours and make a bundle? Why shouldn't you play that way, and be a rich man as long as you live?"

I told them. To start with, casino gambling is a lot like scuba diving. You can only keep it up for a short period of time, if you want to keep your brain working. And if you are playing my system you must keep your head clear.

If you think it's tough reading a paper with someone looking over your shoulder, try concentrating on cards, and mathematics, with twenty or more people hanging on your every move — together with the din of the casino in your ear.

I told the *Telegram* executives that I planned to share the system, to set it down in a book.

I knew I'd never starve as long as I remembered the formula—and I'll never forget it. Trying to set yourself up for life in one session with my system is like trying to take all the gold out of a mine in one day. It doesn't make sense, and it probably can't be done.

CHAPTER 8

Half a bankroll is worse than none

Several months later, Bruce and I decided to raise $21,000 to finance a trip to the European casinos. We would put up $8,000 and Bruce and I would go to Las Vegas again and stay until we had built the $8,000 into $21,000. This would pay the complete air fare for three people as well as leave us a bankroll of $15,000 to play with.

With this settled, Bruce and I left for Las Vegas again the next day, this time staying at the Castaway Hotel.

After a couple of days, Bruce remarked that it would be good to have his wife along. She had never been to Las Vegas and a holiday would do her the world of good. Without any hesitation, a phone call was made and plans set for Beth to join us the next day.

Bruce spent the next few hours with me at the pool. We decided to call Toronto and have my lawyer, Sydney Silverman, join us for a few days, so that he could see the system for himself. Having completed another long distance call to Mr. Silverman, and got his assurance that he would be arriving the next day, Bruce and I set out to visit the casinos and make some money. We did, to the tune of $900.

The following day Bruce and I were up bright and early looking after various odds and ends and making reservations at some of the clubs where we planned to take Beth and Sydney that evening.

It was another hot day in Vegas, and Bruce left me at the pool while he drove to the airport to pick up Beth. It wasn't long before they joined me at the pool, where we enjoyed a few cocktails before heading out for the big evening ahead.

Our first stop was the Desert Inn where Bruce and I had spent most of our leisure time. While Beth and Bruce sipped a cocktail and listened to the music, I would periodically slip away to the tables and cover our expenses in a matter of a few minutes. Back from one of these ventures Beth remarked to me, "Do you really win all the time?"

"No," I said, "that is, if you mean do I win on each roll of the dice, spin of the wheel or turn of the card. However, I do win all the time in regard to the amount of money I have determined beforehand."

"That's wonderful," she said. "I wish that I could do that."

"It's very simple. Would you like to come to the table with me the next time so that you will see that I am not kidding?"

"Yes, I'd love that," she replied.

Without any further hesitation we slipped from our seats and walked through the lounge to the gambling area, where I proceeded to buy $200 worth of chips and with the little black book ready played a half dozen hands of blackjack until I had won the amount I had decided to make. Having done this, I could see the excitement in Beth's eyes and suggested she play another sequence.

"Oh, yes," she said. "This is wonderful. Fantastic."

Playing for another period of about twenty minutes I completed an additional three sequences, having made a profit of some $80. Seated at the bar, I began to explain the story of the system and our experiences over the last three weeks.

I enjoyed a delicious dinner and left Bruce and Beth while I drove to the airport to meet the flight from Chicago carrying our new guest, Sydney Silverman. After stopping at our hotel, we drove to the Dunes Hotel, where we had reservations to see the floor show.

When I started to play I had only half of my bankroll with me. This proved to be a drastic mistake.

As we walked through the lobby of the hotel, I asked Sydney if he would like some spending money. I went to the crap table and won $50. After joining Bruce and Beth in the cocktail lounge we watched the floor show and then decided to catch another show at one of the other clubs. As we were walking out of the lounge past the gambling tables I decided to play some roulette. Since everyone was anxious to see the system in operation again, I purchased $500 worth of chips.

When I started to play I had only half of my bankroll with me. The balance was in the cashier's office at the Desert Inn. This proved to be a drastic mistake.

As I mentioned earlier, it is not a good idea to play the system unless you are carrying every cent of the bankroll in your pocket. It is possible that for a day, a week, or a month, you may only have to use a small portion of your bankroll to make money, but you never know when you will need the full amount.

As I continued to play, I experienced some losses as I varied my bets from red to black and odd to even. I was not aware at the time, due possibly to the excitement of the evening, that I was playing a sequence far beyond the limit my bankroll allowed, and after a period of twenty minutes or so I lost the sum of $2,200.

Once I realized the dreadful mistake I had made, I left the table. After securing more money that we had left in the cashier's office at the Desert Inn, I proceeded to regain my losses.

At one point during the three-day holiday, Sydney and I decided to play blackjack. It was not very long before I realized that Sydney was a babe in the woods when playing blackjack, for as I was playing the system and betting far greater amounts than he, I was losing more than I thought necessary. Why? Sydney was drawing cards for no apparent reason at all and busting himself out as well as everyone at the table.

On my instructions, Sydney then allowed me to play his cards. At the end of one hour I had regained my losses and showed a profit of over $350. As we left the table, Sydney said, "How come *you* made a large profit — and even though you were playing my cards, you lost $60 of my money?"

"Don't worry, Sydney, I'll regain your losses for you at once," I replied. "I was just using your hand as a dummy to beat the dealer."

"But I don't understand," he mumbled.

"Well," I continued, "you were playing your cards and not realizing when to stop and when to draw. The result was that you were busting not only yourself but the other players at the table as well. A lot of the cards you drew should have been passed to the dealer who, in turn, would have lost, allowing us all to win. When I took over playing your cards you noticed that your bets were always $5 and no more?"

"That's right," he answered. "But why?"

"Because I was not concerned about winning or losing with your hand. Your bets were $5 while my bets were $50 and $100. I was letting the dealer draw the cards that you had been drawing, and even though you lost on your hand, the other players and I were winning."

Beth, Bruce and Sydney returned to Toronto leaving me behind to increase the bankroll for our trip to Europe.

CHAPTER 9

I had overstayed my welcome

It was quite apparent that I was now becoming very well known in all the casinos in Las Vegas and I was aware of many eyes watching me as I continued to play, making it much more difficult to concentrate as well as spend a period of more than a few minutes at each table.

It was on one of these visits a few nights later that the tables started to turn for me, and much for the worse. I had started to play at the blackjack table with only a few dollars in front of me, trying to feel out the table without drawing too much attention. I was winning and losing as normal, and at the same time carrying on a conversation with the dealer who seemed quite polite and friendly. After a period of fifteen minutes the dealer was changed and I started to win more frequently. Meanwhile, the first dealer was having a heated discussion with one of the pit bosses off to the side. In ten minutes' time, after I had won $300, the new dealer was replaced. My sixth sense warned me that something was up — I could see that this fellow was very businesslike and even refused to talk, busying himself with the work at hand (which I found out two days later was manipulating the cards) so that he had no time for conversation, only concentration.

As I continued to play I lost the money I

had won. Still losing, and with the dealer unchanged after two hours, I realized that things were not as one would expect. At this point I was down $2,300.

Leaving the table, I proceeded to another casino, where, after a few minutes of play, and winning, the dealer was changed and I started to lose far more hands than the theory of probability would suggest. Leaving that table I decided to call it a night, still unaware that the wheels against me had been set in motion.

The word was out to break me.

The following day I set out once again only to find that each time I started to play the dealers would be changed, and then I would run a streak of heavy losses. During all this time I had been playing blackjack, where the dealer deals the cards from his hands and not from a shoe. It was not until a few days later that a friend who worked in one of the casinos took me aside and explained that the word was out to break me. Vegas had tolerated my presence there for over four months, entertaining people from Canada as well as people I had met there, and paying all my expenses from the profits from the tables. They were becoming a little provoked and decided that to break me financially meant that they would be rid of me. My friend also spent an hour showing the numerous ways that they can manipulate the cards, so fast that even an experienced eye has difficulty spotting it. At the time I was a little skeptical. Today, I realize that psychological ploys and quick-handed dealers alike are used to stop a consistent winner.

I had overstayed my welcome, had become a nuisance. Perhaps the final straw had been when I threw a dinner party for eleven people in the Cactus Room. At the conclusion of dinner the bill was presented, and one of the group remarked that although he thought the cost was high, he realized that the casino would eventually pay for it. And would I be good enough to show them how I played at the tables with the system? Everyone agreed that this would be wonderful so off we went to the tables. By playing for a few moments at blackjack, roulette, and craps I made the dinner cheque in a matter of less than fifteen minutes, while everyone gathered around the table including the casino staff. I don't think that they appreciated the show I put on.

CHAPTER 10

Europe — Where the green felt's greener

The Big Trip was all set up — Bruce and I were to meet at Malton and take off for Europe, the birthplace of the casino. Europe — the land where broke gigolos became millionaires on a spin of the wheel — and millionaires walk quietly into the casino gardens to blow their brains out after another spin of the wheel.

We'd booked a flight to Lisbon on August 5 — an economy move to put us just outside the peak travel season when fares are high.

We had a moderate bankroll, and our itinerary was all figured out. First we'd hit Estorile — a small town twenty miles from Lisbon. Then Nice, Monte Carlo and Cannes. There were five gambling towns to sample in Germany — then across the channel to London, one of the newer legal gambling cities in the world.

The flight took us first to Madrid. Dawn was painting the leading edge of the wings when we woke. I looked out on brilliant blue sea, separated by a slash of white from the brown earth of Spain.

We took a cab downtown, and strolled around Madrid. I don't know what I was expecting — but Old Spain I didn't see. The homes — yes. They were Spanish through and through. There were even a few people dozing on doorsteps in the 80° sun.

But all around—everywhere—there were high-rise apartments and office buildings, in all stages of completion. They didn't even look like Spanish apartments should look.

We hadn't much time to savor or criticize Madrid. We caught our flight to Lisbon — and a minor panic.

Bruce is a big, good-looking fellow. We were headed for the little bus that would take us from the plane to the air terminal building, when a stewardess saw him. "That's Kirk Douglas — I'm sure it's Kirk Douglas," she fairly trumpeted.

We made the bus a millimetre or so ahead of the drove of females who charged at Bruce when they heard the clarion call. I was glad to be aboard the bus. Bruce gave me a funny look. To this day, I don't know whether he was happy about missing the thrill of being Kirk Douglas for a few seconds.

They lost our bags at the terminal. They shipped them back to Madrid by mistake.

Hardened to this sort of thing by now, we rented a car and drove the thirty kilometres to the Grande Hotel in Estoril.

No luggage meant no shave, so we didn't try the casino that night. I wasn't about to launch my European gambling venture with a stubbly chin.

We spent the next day and night loafing — for the bags still hadn't arrived.

Good for the morale.

I heard a story once about a British officer in the trenches of France, in the First World War. Despite the mud, blood and shrapnel, he'd send his men one at a time into the dugout for a shave. "Good for the morale," he'd explain to any superior who noticed the idle rifle at the parapet. And his squad proved he was right. They fought harder and longer than the rest.

I'm with him. The shave and general clean-up that our luggage made possible gave us a new view of Europe.

Hours before, the dining room waiters looked at us as though they were pondering whether it was worth getting their hands dirty to throw these two obvious bums out.

But now, when we made our grand entrance, we felt sure all eyes were on the two sparkling, debonair playboys who were honoring the room.

We ate, walked a quarter of a mile down a tree-lined street, and stood at the edge of a beautiful garden. Beyond the garden, discreet lettering proclaimed a large building the "Estoril Casino." This was the start of a new adventure.

CHAPTER 11

New problems in the Old World

Before they let us into the gaming room, we were required to fill out identification cards, and show our passports.

The gaming room was crowded. Packed. I changed $2,000 into escudos, and sat down at the roulette wheel. A liveried youth approached me, a cloth bag over his shoulder. This was the Portuguese method of selling chips. The chips are rectangular — and the higher the denomination, the thicker and longer the chip.

I started to play, and promptly plunged toward fiscal suicide.

It's easy to bet with dollars and cents. But try translating 28.6 escudos to the dollar, which was the exchange rate back in the early 1960's, and chaos sets in rapidly.

The chips were all in multiples of five escudos. So if my system told me the bet should be, say, $36, I'd have to bet 1,008 escudos—and they just don't have 8-escudo chips. I was soon running short of money — so I joined Bruce in the cocktail lounge, to take stock. I figured it out quickly and the news was bad. I'd been betting up to five times more than I should have been betting, because of the difference between the dollars and the escudos.

Back at the hotel we assessed our position.

It wasn't desperate — but it was awfully close to it.

We had $685 left from our bankroll. This left us three choices: (a) Go home to Canada on our prepaid tickets, (b) wire home for money — from God knows whom, or (c) try to carry on with what was left of the money.

I knew that I had failed and that the system hadn't. And I still have a little adventure left in my soul. So we decided to press on.

Nice is like a dignified Las Vegas.

We flew to Nice the next morning. It would take literary power far beyond mine to describe the Riviera. The colors are incredible. The sea is pure and blue. The sandy beaches are so white they hurt the eye, yet not so white as the sparkling villas that overlook the Mediterranean.

We walked about an hour before we found a hotel to suit our pocketbooks. It was about a four-minute walk from the casino, so our luck wasn't all bad.

Nice is like a dignified Las Vegas. The casinos don't scream at you. They invite you — quietly, persuasively.

The first one we entered was the Casino de Mediterranean, nestled between two shiny hotels. We bought a membership card and walked up to a game called seven-to-one.

This was a lot like roulette, but with a bigger wheel. The wheel is like a shallow inverted cone, and the wheelman sets a little ball rolling around the edge. It spirals into one of a series of holes near the bottom.

We watched this for a while, then looked at the roulette and baccarat. We couldn't play, because, as it was a warm evening, we'd left our suitcoats at the hotel. A suitcoat and a tie is a must in European casinos. They like taking the sucker's money as much as they do in Vegas — but they do it with so much more decorum.

We also learned that in Europe the casinos close from 5 AM to 1 PM. In Vegas they're open round the clock.

Next day, shortly after opening time, we went to the Casino Municipale. I surveyed the games and played for half an hour on the roulette wheel. I left $73 richer. I was getting better at converting our money into foreign currency.

We went over to the Casino de Mediterranean — and the wheel there gave me another $84.

It was late afternoon, and the hot sun was turning the Mediterranean into a sheet of molten gold. We'd been winning, and felt good.

Monte Carlo is the Mecca of gamblers.

We decided to head right away for the most famous casino town of them all — Monte Carlo.

Monte Carlo has to be the cleanest town in the world. The buildings are sparkling white, with dazzling colored roof-tiles laying a patchwork of rainbow over the pristine streets.

The casino is set, like a temple, in one of the loveliest gardens I've ever seen. Colored lights were twinkling under the trees in the dusk. Magic. That was the word for it.

Inside — majestic opulence. Everywhere there was rich brocade and marble. The whole interior seemed to be carved from aged white marble. Monte Carlo is the Mecca of gamblers.

Perhaps that's why the casino gave me the

feeling of being in a shrine. They have a private escort to take you individually to the gaming room by private elevator. They make you feel like a prince.

In the gaming room, on the second floor, I found the first crap table I'd seen in Europe. But I decided to stick with roulette and I picked up $180 in about twenty minutes.

European roulette is played differently from the American game. The European game gives the player a slight edge, because there are fewer ways to lose money on a spin. But the edge, as always, is with the house. The European wheel has one green, while the American wheel has two. Most European casinos now have American wheels as well as the native variety.

We returned to Nice and paid one more visit to the Casino Municipale the following day before flying to Stuttgart, Germany. From Stuttgart, it's a hundred mile drive to Baden-Baden and the nearest casino.

In Germany it isn't a casino. It's a Spielbank. But only the name is different. The Spielbank was very much like the other casinos we'd seen in Europe. Except, perhaps, that it was richer in decor than even Monte Carlo. Bright red rugs, gold chandeliers and gold statuettes.

The casino was beautiful — the roulette wheel contributed $105 to our bankroll — but when we quit, we found the weakness of Baden-Baden. In the wee hours of the morning, a hungry gambler can't buy as much as a ham sandwich.

We spent the following morning like a pair of average tourists — taking pictures, mostly of each other, with bits of Germany peeking over our shoulders.

Out of film, we drove to Bad Homburg, fifteen miles north of Frankfurt. The casino which contributed handsomely to our kitty, is one of the oldest in Europe.

Our next stop was Wiesbaden, a casino town thirty miles to the west.

We drove into town, and asked for directions to the casino.

We drove down broad streets, then narrower streets, and finally up what was little more than a lane.

It smelled funny, and the building didn't look like any of the other casinos. It was old and run down. We went in, and down a hall. It smelled of sauerkraut and garlic. We wound up in a dingy room with a table. There were five men and a dealer playing poker at the table.

Hesitantly, I asked if this was the casino.

When they had stopped laughing they told us we'd either been given wrong directions or had taken a wrong turn. The real action, they explained through heavy Teutonic accents, was four miles away.

One of them drew a rough map — and in half an hour we were in another Spielbank. The Wiesbaden casino is very old, very quiet and very crowded. Strangely, the quiet of the place bothered me. We only stayed an hour, then drove to Bad Neuenahr, south of Bonn, another one hundred and ten miles.

It was nearly three in the morning and the entire town was in darkness. Except for the casino. As we pulled our rented Opel between the Rolls Royces and Mercedes on the parking lot, I remember feeling very good about life in general. Since the first unfortunate incident at Estoril, we had averaged between $100 and $125 per casino.

This one was no exception. The roulette wheel contributed $136 to the cause in twenty-five minutes.

That same morning we caught a plane for Hamburg and with another car drove to Travelmunde on the Baltic coast. We couldn't find accommodation in the resort town so we decided to commute from Hamburg.

In Hamburg, for the first time since we arrived in Europe, we made some friends. Hans and Ursula Korner became our guides for the visit, and made our stay in Hamburg the most pleasant episode in our European tour.

The casino at Travelmunde did its bit to make the visit enjoyable too.

But we had to press on and we caught our first glimpse of London, predictably, through a fog.

We checked into the Mayfair Hotel, one of the most exclusive, just because we felt like pampering ourselves a bit.

On our first night we played at the River Club, Aspinals, Adeurs and Cockfords, separating each from a few quid. Next night, it was the new Victoria, the Olympic, the 21, Les Ambes, Quintos and Brookes. We spent the days like tourists — Buckingham Palace, Westminster Abbey, The Tower and so forth. At night we cleaned up at the casinos. The London stop was the most profitable of the tour by far.

Gambling in Europe is looked on as more of a true sport.

The London clubs open at eight in the evening and stay open until 3 or 4 AM. Like the rest of the European clubs, the atmosphere is relaxed and friendly. There's none of the mind-jarring noise and confusion of Las Vegas. There's none of the deadly seriousness that underlies Las Vegas gambling.

Gambling in Europe is looked on as more of a true sport. If you win — Whoopee. If you lose — C'est la vie.

By the time we got on the plane for Toronto we had visited twenty-one casinos. We'd performed this feat with the incredibly small bankroll of $300, which was all we had left after expenses when we left Estoril.

Our expenses on the trip — and we hadn't cut any corners — came to nearly $3,000. Our $300 bankroll paid for all this, and got us back to Toronto with the $300 still intact — and a $72 profit.

Our trip was a success, I'm sure, only because we didn't spend much time in any one casino. I'm convinced that this is a good rule to follow in Nevada, Europe or the Bahamas. You save yourself a lot of grief by not giving the house time to muster what hidden talents it may have to combat consistent winners.

Small profits — quick returns.

CHAPTER 12

The supreme test

I was still submitting myself to every conceivable test suggested by people who did not believe the system could work. Each test was to be the last, the supreme test. However, the line of supreme tests became endless. As I met new people, new challenges were suggested with the hope of breaking the system.

As a test to end all tests, I decided to take a group of strangers to the Bahamas. The plan was as follows: letters would be sent to people who had written to me after having viewed one of my television performances, suggesting that they put up $1,000. For this I would take them on a five-day, all-expenses-paid holiday to the Grand Bahama Island. I would use their money for a bankroll and at the conclusion of the trip, return their initial investment of $1,000 plus a profit of $100.

I selected the people whom I thought would be interested and sent the following letter to them as well as a copy of the itinerary planned by the travel agency which has handled the majority of my trips to all parts of the world.

Dear . . .

In consideration of your interest as shown in your letter of May 29th, I have selected you along with fourteen others to be my guest for an all expenses paid five day holiday to the Grand Bahama Islands.

For the sum of $1,000, I am prepared to pay your air fare return, hotel and meals for five days from Thursday, September 15th to Monday, September 19th, when we shall visit Nassau and Freeport.

Upon our return you shall be repaid your initial investment of $1,000, plus 10% interest on your money. If you would like to take your wife, the expenses incurred will be your responsibility and will be approximately $200.

You will be escorted to the Bahama Club in Nassau and the Lucayan Beach Hotel and the Monte Carlo Casino in Freeport.

There are many other interesting sights as well as facilities for golfing, boating and a skeet and trap shooting range, deep sea fishing and best of all a duty free port.

As you know I have visited over sixty casinos throughout the world, and it has been decided that I should select fifteen complete strangers from all walks of life to travel with me and visit casinos, so that I may add additional validity to the fact that the method does work. You may be requested to give a testimonial as to your opinion of the method.

For the $1,000 you will invest prior to our departure you will receive the following:
1. Your $1,000 investment plus a bonus of $100.
2. Air fare return to Toronto.
3. Four days accommodation plus meals.
4. A free round of skeet or trap shooting.
5. A fishing trip called bottom fishing.

6. A cocktail party prior to our leaving for home.
7. Group discussion regarding systems and how to apply them.

If you think this is a wonderful and fascinating opportunity and are agreeable to join me for our departure on September 15th, please send your reply immediately to be received no later than August 30th, as shortness of time necessitates early response so that final arrangements can be made.

Trusting I may have the pleasure of both you and your wife joining me for a delightful holiday and a closer look at casino gambling.

Yours sincerely,
A. B. Irwin

On September 15, we all arranged to meet at the Toronto International Airport, to catch the Nassau flight. My group consisted of Mr. and Mrs. Richard Scarzo of Warren, Michigan; Mr. and Mrs. Sam Scarzo of Detroit, Michigan; Miss Betty Hoffman of Montreal, Quebec; Mr. Robert Gill of Bowmanville, Ontario; Mr. Harry Greenberg, of Toronto, Ontario; Mr. and Mrs. B. Baxter, of Scarborough, Ontario and myself.

Our plans were to spend two nights in Nassau at the Montague Beach Hotel, which is about twenty-five minutes drive to the Bahama Club where they have legalized gambling. Realizing that many of these people had never been to a gambling casino before, I decided to make my stay slightly longer so that they would have the opportunity of enjoying the action at the tables, as well as playing the slot machines. I had picked the crap table to play at this particular evening and had decided upon making $1,000 that night.

Two-and-a-half hours later I had my $1,000 and decided it was time to have a drink.

While I was playing at the table the rest of the group were walking around enjoying themselves, some playing the slots and periodically dropping over to the crap table to see how I was doing. Two-and-a-half hours later I had my $1,000 and decided it was time to have a drink. As I was cashing my chips in, the manager of the casino asked if I would care to eat, compliments of the house. I mentioned to him that I was travelling with a group of people, and immediately he suggested that they all join me for dinner in their main dining room. It has a very romantic atmosphere, with soft violin music, which we enjoyed very much. Once seated, the manager told us we could order anything we wished. We all enjoyed a delicious steak dinner washed down with bottles of champagne.

We returned to our hotel. The next morning we spent shopping and sight-seeing throughout Nassau, picking up souvenirs for our friends back home.

That afternoon we relaxed and soaked up the sun around the pool. That evening we dressed and met in the main dining room. As it was still too early to visit the casino, we adjourned to the cocktail lounge. Here we whiled away another delightful hour or two. Junie James, a professional singer and violinist who was sitting with our group in the lounge, was asked by the hotel management to sing a few songs, which were greatly enjoyed by everyone present. To show their appreciation the hotel supplied us with bottle after bottle of free champagne until 12:30 in the morning. When the last drop of champagne had disappeared we recruited three taxis to take us to the casino. Once there, I told our group that I would be playing for only fifteen minutes, due to the late hour. In less than that time, I had added an additional $1,500 to the $1,000 we had won the night before.

At the end of the two hours we departed the casino with another $1,100 profit.

The following morning was a Saturday and our itinerary called for us to leave Nassau and take a thirty-five minute flight to the Grand Bahama Island. We stayed at the luxurious Oceanus Hotel, directly across from the Lucayan Beach Hotel, where the gambling casino is situated. After touring the island in our rented Volkswagen bus we took a dip at the pool and dressed for dinner. At 10:30 that evening we left the Oceanus, and took the two minute walk to the casino in the fabulous Lucayan Beach Hotel. During the next two hours I moved from table to table, varying my bets according to my system. At the end of the two hours we departed the casino with another $1,100 profit.

The next day the group had the opportunity of deep sea fishing, golfing, or skeet shooting. We took a vote, loaded the bus and headed for the skeet range. That evening, our last, we spent another two hours gambling, where I picked up a profit of $4,100. The following day we flew from the Grand Bahama Island to Nassau and caught the 7:00 PM flight to Toronto.

The bottom line? $1,000, $1,500, $1,100, $4,100 — in other words, $1,500 for the guests, another $6,200 for their host.

CHAPTER 13

Case histories

Monday, April 19th, started off like any other Monday; like any other Monday there was the usual pile up of paperwork; the usual grumpy Monday morning back-to-workers; and the usual telephone calls from customers in trouble . . . then a call from a customer who wasn't in trouble, just calling socially to invite me to his apartment for the evening. This invitation was the beginning of the most unusual experience of my life.

On arriving at Ron Dunn's apartment, I was introduced to Bruce Irwin, a genial sort of fellow whom I liked at once, but on being told he had a "system" for beating the gambling tables, I immediately became wary, and said I would have to be shown—and shown I was.

Now, I am no gambler! The truth is I have never had any inclination to play cards or craps or any other gambling games that appeal to so many men. I point this out only to show that it wasn't any gambling bug or fever that appealed to me in this situation. No—as the evening wore on I could see that this system was really "no gamble." Bruce literally, on paper, made me a bundle.

To prove his system "under fire," he suggested that I put up a bankroll of $5,000. With this we would go to Las Vegas and endeavor to double our money. "Aha," you say as everyone else did, "now this 'con man' begins to show his spots." However, I was as impressed with the man as I was with the system, and although I am no gambler with cards, I was willing to take a chance on Bruce. Also, as it is my contention that "he who hesitates is lost," I told him to make the reservations for our flight to Las Vegas the next afternoon.

Our first stop was the cashiers wicket in the casino to convert our traveller's cheques into cash. This posed no problem and from this I handed Bruce a considerable sum and told him to "go and make our air fare." I might point out here that Bruce always has a goal in mind when he starts his system; a specific amount he plans to make. This is what keeps the system successful. Bruce made over $145 towards our air fare in a matter of a few minutes.

For the rest of our stay I enjoyed myself with the sights and sounds of this town of fabulous entertainment, Bruce continued to make money to cover all expenses. This included hotel, meals, car rentals, floor shows, and even articles of clothing. Because of business commitments, I had to return to Toronto at the weekend—not without some regret.

Two weeks later, accompanied by three prominent Toronto businessmen who were most interested in seeing this "impossible" system work, we returned to Las Vegas. This time we registered at the Desert Inn and were greeted most cordially. While the rest of us swam in the pool, played golf, and generally played the tourist even to losing a little at the gambling tables, Bruce Irwin would periodically go to the gambling tables and easily make the money to cover the expenses for all of us.

Bruce would go to the tables without any hesitation or concern. Of course he was not concerned — he knows his system never fails. This easy living went on for four days and, then, home to Toronto and reality.

It seemed now that everyone in Toronto wanted to have the system proved to them, so two weeks later Bruce invited a lawyer to accompany us. This trip was no different than the last. We all had a fine time, although I was realizing more and more why Bruce could not sit at the tables and play and win for any length of time. I am sure the noise and confusion of the hundreds of people around, and the music from the bars made it difficult to concentrate. Also, the croupiers and the pit-bosses governing the tables could be changed at will once they discovered that Bruce really was a winner. This meant he had to make the amount he had decided on, and move on. However, to my amazement, he could even fool these practiced gamblers. It was possible for him to drop money at one table and, using his system, pick up the sequence at another table and, as usual, come out the winner.

Bruce Baxter

As a commentary on Bruce Irwin's gambling methods — I hesitate to use the word "system" since virtually all the mathematical authorities agree there is no such thing as a fool-proof system — all I can say is this: In a week of observing Mr. Irwin at various Las Vegas gambling casinos last April, I never once saw him lose. This is, he

never left a table a loser, although of course,
he did lose on some throws of the dice or
turns of the card at Blackjack.

In repeated demonstrations during which
he set a "win objective" each time, Mr. Irwin
came through with the exact winning amount.
These were mostly fairly small wins from $10
up to, on one occasion, $245. It was an
impressive display.

Arthur Cole

I accompanied Bruce Irwin to Las Vegas
in May 1965 and saw Bruce use his gambling
system at the Roulette Wheel, the Crap table
and Blackjack table. Bruce won $50 for me at
the Crap table which I had personally lost and
after losing it again he again won the money
back for me.

I enjoyed marvellous entertainment as
well as the excellent food. After leaving the
dining room one evening in particular the
total of the bill was $166 for the five in our
party. Bruce Irwin took me to the Blackjack
table and in a matter of minutes won $150
toward the bill. We then walked over to the
Crap table to make the other $16 and it was at
this point that I saw him lose money many
times in a row costing us $1,000. The $1,000
was won back fifteen minutes later as well as
our $16 profit.

His system worked at all tables as far as I
could see and we received $600 plus expenses
paid for our investment of $1,700 each.

Doug Cole

I have witnessed the most fantastic and
baffling display of a gambling system in my
lifetime.

Bruce Irwin has lived up to his end of our agreement by using gambling winnings to pay for this trip and has more than fulfilled, to date, his arrangement with me.

It is my considered opinion that he has a "system" which works and does so consistently.

This experience has been one which I will long remember.

Robert J. Gill

Taking the opportunity to write this testimonial was more than a pleasure. I only wish that all of you had had the opportunity to travel with Mr. Irwin. My wife and I had unforgettable pleasures. It was like a second honeymoon for us. Only this time it was free of charge. We flew from Toronto, Canada to Nassau. We stayed in Nassau 2½ days and Freeport, Grand Bahama Island 2½ days. This included all our expenses starting with air fare, hotel, food, skiing, boating, skeet shooting, deep sea fishing, cocktails and dancing, and including tipping the maids, waiters and bell hops.

Mr. Irwin never failed to answer questions that confronted him the whole time we were there. He based the purpose of the trip on, "I will win and pay all your expenses while in the Bahamas." Planning this trip was a lot of work on his part. I will say, that while in the casinos watching Mr. Irwin gamble, we could see the calmness and confidence that he expressed while gambling were proof that using his controlled method of gambling, regardless of the time, he would leave the casino winning the exact amount that he predicted before going in.

Surely, if I went on any further I could write a book of our experience with the man called "Midas."

Mr. & Mrs. Richard Scarzo

We left Toronto on October 10, 1966. I returned on October 24th. Here is a brief run-down of our casino visits in London, England. Tuesday evening we visited the Victoria Sporting Club. This night was extremely disappointing to me and I began to doubt that his system would work. He lost £140 and while we were leaving the casino, Bruce explained to me that the limit, which was £30, was too low. He said we would go only to casinos where the limit was £100 or more.

Wednesday evening at the Palm Beach Club, where the limit was £100, he made exactly £200 between ten and twelve minutes.

Thursday evening we visited the George Raft Colony Club, and in twenty minutes made £75. The same evening our second stop was the Golden Nugget where he collected £50. The third stop the same evening was the Pigalle Club, where Bruce made £206 at craps. As we were leaving we stopped at the Blackjack table and between the two of us we made a quick £42.

There were evenings when Bruce gave me money and was beside me and told me what to do. At one club they changed dealers on us three times in ten minutes. They knew something was going on, but we did not stay long enough for them to figure out what it was.

On Friday evening Bruce collected £225 at the Palm Beach Club. Saturday evening it was £170 profit from the Olympic Sporting

Club.

On Friday, October 21st, we resumed gambling at the Palm Beach Club, where Bruce picked up £55.

Saturday evening we visited the George Raft Colony Club once again and within five minutes Bruce had lost £1,000. We left the craps table and I suggested that we leave and go to another club. He assured me that going to another club would not make any difference and said: "I'll get the £1,000 back, plus a profit, but it's going to take me two or three hours to do it." At 4 o'clock in the morning he had won his £1,000 back and £212 profit. The management invited us for dinner the next evening, but we asked if we could have breakfast. We had breakfast and returned to the hotel at 5:00 AM.

Sunday evening we went to the Golden Nugget Club where Bruce won £260 in twenty minutes. We had friends from London with us that evening. One of them was performing at a cabaret club. After Bruce had won the £260 he wanted to know how much dinner would cost at the cabaret. Our friend said: "About £20." Bruce pulled out a handful of chips from his pocket and said: "I had better go to the table and make £20 for dinner." He did this within five minutes and we were off to the cabaret for dinner and entertainment.

Most casinos serve drinks free of charge to those gambling, but Bruce has a rule that he does not drink until after he has finished at the tables.

We saw one man lose £2,000 in five rolls of the dice. This is only one example of many people we saw lose hundreds and thousands of pounds.

The Saturday evening when Bruce dropped
£1,000, he had lost twenty-nine straight times
before getting back on the winning streak.
With his system, he knows he will always win.
Calmness and a big bankroll are necessary at
all times.

In this two-week period, Bruce Irwin
made $3,897.

William Whiting

One of the most extraordinary nights I have
ever experienced involved a professional
gambler by the name of Bruce Irwin.

I became associated with Irwin, then
forty-one, a Canadian, after Hughie Green had
asked me to appear on his television show,
The Sky's the Limit, in April 1972. Hughie
explained that Irwin had already been on
the programme and won £100 answering
questions on geography. They had also talked
about a book Irwin had written in which he
claimed to have a system of winning at
roulette and other gambling games. He was
returning to the programme the following
week to hand over his winnings — if any — to
charity, plus the original £100 stake money,
i.e., the £100 he had won answering the
questions correctly. Hughie wanted me to go
with the Canadian gambler to a London
casino and return with him to the show to
describe what had happened. "What if he
loses?" I asked Hughie. "You come on just the
same and say so."

The *Mirror* gave me the go-ahead to take
part in the exercise and I met Irwin at the
Londonderry House in Park Lane. He turned
out to be a typical hustler; a Mississippi
gambler in the true Hollywood tradition;

trousers with large cheeks; two-toned shoes and a tie which looked as though someone had thrown a raw egg at it.

Irwin told me he was about to launch a book describing his gambling methods, hence his appearance on the Hughie Green show. The book was called *The Midas Touch* and 11,000 copies had been sold in Canada and America. It was now being marketed in Britain at £5 a copy.

Bruce Irwin, not without a sense of humour, was a very smooth talker. He answered all my questions and although I wasn't too impressed with his gambling system, which turned out to be a method of staking, I was intrigued to learn that he had been banned by four London casinos because of his winnings.

"First of all," I told him, "Let's go to one of these casinos where they won't let you in."

We walked around the corner to the Park Lane Casino and, sure enough, Irwin was refused entry. No reason was given. The receptionist just refused admittance and when someone from the management arrived he too confirmed they didn't want Irwin in their club. They were, of course, perfectly entitled to turn him away but this made me all the more keen to see gambler Bruce in action.

We then went to the Playboy Club. Here his reception was entirely the opposite: drinks were on the house and so was our meal. To them, Irwin was something of a celebrity. He was good for business. His mere presence at the gaming tables drew a crowd. And, if Bruce was to be believed, the Playboy management welcomed him because he could always prove that you can win — if you know how.

We had had a couple of drinks and eaten our meal. Bruce was telling more tales of his gambling coups but I was beginning to get restless.

"It's all very well telling me about all your wins but when are you going to show me just how you do it?"

Irwin then took the £100 from his inside breast pocket and gave it to an attendant to change into £10 chips. He sauntered over to the roulette table, put down a couple of £10 chips, watched the ball spin, picked up three chips . . . and walked away.

"There you are," he said. "That's it."

"That's what?"

"That's it. I won £10."

This was my first visit to a London casino and after all the tales Irwin had been telling I was not all impressed with his £10 win. He pointed out that he had secured ten per cent tax-free income on his £100 stake in a few seconds, whereas people normally had to wait a whole twelve months for such a return and pay tax as well. I challenged him to repeat what he had just done. We walked back to the game, he put down two chips, and he won again. Now he was £20 up on his original investment.

"Don't tell me you have written a whole book telling people how to win at roulette just by doing that?"

"Not really. I have that staking system I told you about. That's what I sell with the book. What I've shown you is a very simple method of making a quick return on your bankroll. But you mustn't be greedy — take ten per cent profit and then quit."

Irwin then went on to explain to me exactly what he had done. It wasn't foolproof and you wouldn't make a fortune, but if you wanted to gamble then it was better to have some sort of system or pattern for your play instead of putting down chips in a haphazard way. His ten per cent return had been achieved by putting a chip on two of the centre columns but leaving the third column alone. This gave him odds of two-to-one. In other words he had two columns of numbers going for him and only one column plus zero against.

Like most gamblers, he also followed the wheel. If on the previous spin the ball had lodged on a red number then he would place his two chips on columns one and three which, between them, have the most red numbers. If the ball had slotted into a black number then he would back columns one and two since in these blacks predominate. Sometimes he would gamble against the wheel, i.e., if black came up he would place his two chips on the two columns with the most red numbers (one and three); if red then it would be one and two which have the most black.

Next week I was back on *The Sky's the Limit* with Bruce Irwin and I told viewers exactly what had happened.

"Don't you think it very unfair that a London casino should ban our Canadian friend?" demanded quizmaster Hughie, indignantly.

"I certainly do."

But no one asked me just how Irwin had won the money at the Playboy Club so I didn't have to reveal his system.

Before we went on the show I'd suggested to Bruce that he donate the money to a fund which had been set up in London to help Al Koran, the British magician, who was seriously ill in America. He was agreeable and it was announced on the show. I later sent off a cheque for £120 to the fund.

As we motored back to London from Yorkshire Television's studios in Leeds, Bruce told me many tales of his gambling experiences. Finally I challenged him: "If you're so sure of success, why don't you and I go gambling one night? We'll put up a bankroll between us and share the winnings."

"Okay," Irwin replied, "but I'll need a large amount. I'll put up £2,000. Will you do the same?"

I gulped a little, but I wasn't going to back out at this stage. I dropped him off at the Mayfair Hotel (where he always stayed—in the Monte Carlo Suite) and a meeting was arranged for later in the week. Before we met, Irwin phoned to say he had done a check at Foyle's, Harrod's and other London stores stocking his book. Sales had improved considerably following his TV appearance. I began to think that maybe there was something in this gambling business after all.

The night for our gambling spree arrived and we went to the International Sportsmen's Club in Tottenham Court Road. Irwin, who liked to do everything in style, had hired a Rolls complete with security guard to take care of our £4,000 cash, plus any winnings that were to come.

We started at roulette. He turned the cash into chips and great piles of these went on the two columns. Not being a gambler I couldn't follow everything that was happening but I did hear Irwin say to the pit-boss: "Raise the limit?" The man nodded and the next moment Irwin was walking away.

"That's it," he said. "We've done it."

"Done what?"

"Won, of course. That's what we came for isn't it?"

He then went on to play blackjack — on his own. He was phenomenal. He liked to take the whole table and play all five hands. Not every casino will permit this. There was quite a crowd watching him and by the time he'd finished he'd won well over £1,000. The security man cashed our chips and when we were back in the Monte Carlo Suite, Irwin gave me my share of the roulette winnings plus my £2,000 stake. He'd won £750 for me.

We split a bottle of champagne, for which I paid. It seemed the least I could do. But there was just one point I wanted cleared up before I left him:

"You know when you asked the pit-boss to raise the limit . . . you were losing then, weren't you?"

"Yes," nodded the gambler. "We were losing."

"How much?"

"Twelve hundred pounds."

"And half of that money was mine?"

"Of course, I thought you knew that."

I knew it all right but it wasn't until that moment the full impact of what I had staked really hit me. I went home, showered the notes all over the kitchen and bought a new fridge. Apart from an odd pound or two, I've never gambled since.

Clifford Davis, Columnist for the Daily Mirror

CHAPTER 14

My test aboard the Hudson

Slowly I inched along with the other travellers aboard the late morning Toronto to Montreal flight. Between the little girl in front of me kicking up her heels and banging me in the shins and the guy behind me hitting me in the rearend with his bag every few seconds I felt that I would never get to my seat in one piece.

As soon as we were airborne, I recalled that it had only been four or five days previously that I had received a long distance call from the EXPO people in Montreal asking if I was the chap who had played the IBM 1620 computer at the Bayview IBM center back in 1964. Because I had beaten this machine at blackjack for a paper profit of $794 with my mathematical strategy, they wanted me to challenge the computer aboard the Canadian naval ship *Hudson* which was on display at the EXPO grounds. They wanted to show the general public the functioning of the computers and had one programmed to play dice.

So they challenged me to come to Montreal and play against their computer. Without any hesitation I accepted the challenge, with the understanding that they pay for my airfare and hotel accommodation. I knew they had already informed the news media to cover the story.

Upon arriving in Montreal I hastily visited the men's washroom and quickly washed and changed into a business suit I had brought along for an emergency. As I took the taxi to the EXPO grounds I realized that up to this point I had been around the world three times and visited over 400 casinos.

After walking aboard the ship and being introduced to Dr. Smith, who was the co-ordinator and the man in charge, I was given the instructions as to the operation of the computer. In front of this big grey machine was a typewriter. I was instructed to push the "Y" key on the typewriter which immediately put the computer into motion. The first question that it asked me was: "Do you wish to play dice?" I answered yes. The next question was "How old are you?" As long as I pushed any two digits the machine immediately went into operation. First question: "How much do you bet?" After punching in two digits the next question was: "Do you wish to throw the dice?" If you answered yes, the computer continued on. The typewriter started to immediately type out "Player" — "Bank". Under "Player" came the number "4." To activate the next throw of the dice I pushed the keys "Y-U" on the typewriter. The next figure that came up was "9" under Player. Pushing "Y-U" again, the next number that came up was a "6." Again pushing "Y-U" the next number came up "4." Immediately the typewriter would print "You Win — Amount Bet" and the two digits that you had pushed as your bet. Now mind you at this point I must have had around thirty-five news media people as well as other dignitaries both from the universities and various other segments of the ship's personnel. After playing against the computer for approximately forty-five minutes, the typewriter finally typed out *"Congratulations, you* *are the first individual to have broken the bank for $4,092."*

As I turned away from the machine one of the remarks from a professor from the university was that he couldn't believe that anybody could beat the machine for he was the one that was instrumental in programming it. My answer to him was: "If it was programmed by man, it can be beaten by man as well." Although many people came up and congratulated me, I found later, while having dinner at the press club in Montreal with some of the newsmen, that because I consistently seemed to win at every test, I was no longer a newsworthy item.

CHAPTER 15

My introduction into show business

It was back in 1963 that I was introduced to Junie James, a violinist at the Desert Inn Hotel casino in Las Vegas. June and I became very good friends and spent the next five years travelling all over the world sightseeing and paying our expenses from the casinos.

During this period I became extremely interested in the art of magic, and while June and I were in England I spent most of the day-time visiting various magic shows and learning as much about the business as I could. I was introduced to Oliver Godfrey, a gentleman about eighty years of age who had not only been a magician for many years, but also had built the various magical props that a magician needs.

June and I were on an extended tour of Europe so I made arrangements for Oliver to travel with us for the next three months. Each day during that period, he would teach me various magic tricks he had used in nightclubs over the years. During all our travels through Germany, Belgium, France and Italy, we used the casinos to pay our daily expenses. As well, I paid Ollie $50 per day to teach me the tricks of his trade. In 1967 I purchased about $15,000 worth of his magic equipment so that I could put on a full nightclub act, billing myself, "Midas the Magnificent."

Here I was, a man who had the ability to win money consistently in casinos, yet who had a yen to do magic tricks!

On my return to Toronto I went into agent Billy O'Connor's office on Church Street. Billy had placed June into many different little shows that he had going around the city. When I walked into his office and told him that I had returned from Europe where   I had   studied to be a magician, you can imagine how funny he thought the situation was. Here I was, a man who had the ability to win money consistently in casinos, yet who had a yen to do magic tricks! As it happened, Billy was putting together a show for the patients at Toronto General Hospital, and a magic act would be perfect.

The next thing I did was purchase fourteen doves from a friend. Then I spent three days practising, and by Saturday I was as ready as I ever would be. There I was, dressed in my tuxedo, and pushing my trolley out onto the platform. What happened next was pure Marx Brothers comedy. To start with, at the top of my props trolley was a plastic egg, which was to separate in half — magically. The egg was filled with glycerine as well as a yellow plastic yolk. The egg rolled off the top of the cart and onto the floor below the front of the stage, and as I jumped down to pick it up, I managed to cover my hand with the glycerine. When I did get back up on stage, a polite lady in the front row whispered, "Pardon me, son. I think you dropped something." As I gazed down at the front of the stage, I saw two doves and realized that they had fallen out of the pockets in my tux as I had bent over to pick up the egg. Two doves, wrapped up in their little cloth pouches held together with velcro, were looking up at me. I immediately jumped off stage to pick them up, deciding to kneel down this time because I didn't want to lose any more creatures. As I proceeded to kneel down to pick up the two doves, the heels on my shoes tripped two canes that I had attached to my back belt under my tail jacket. Now I had lost five props: one egg, two doves and two canes. Meanwhile, the piano player, who had a note telling him to start the music when he sees a cane appear, is playing like crazy while doves are slipping from my hands and canes are going off in opposite directions! The patients obviously enjoyed the rest of the show, but they never figured out whether it was a magician's act or comedian's act. Nor did the doves, who took six hours of coaxing to descend from the chandeliers.

Actually, no other performance was so unfortunate, and for a couple of years I enjoyed travelling around the city with my magic show. It was only because my consulting work became so demanding that I gave up the act, selling my equipment to a number of magicians in the city. But for two years, June and I enjoyed being showbusiness buddies.

For the next several years, I concentrated on teaching people how to play intelligently in the casinos. I was giving classes in midtown Toronto, corresponding with many people throughout Canada and the United States on all matters related to casino gambling — how to react, how to be a better player, how to control money and so forth — and was introducing a new form of entertainment to the city. This last task involved renting blackjack tables to private corporations that were planning to hold a party; guests could amuse themselves by playing at the tables with "funny money," and at the end of the evening there would be an auction for prizes.

I was also spending a fair bit of time travelling back and forth to London to look after several business interests and to make money at the casinos.

Ray Sonin, a popular Toronto radio host, suggested one day that I produce a show, in Canada, especially for the many British people living there. Vera Lynn, the Forces' Sweetheart, was a good friend of Ray's, and he suggested that the time was right for her to headline a show at Maple Leaf Gardens. I was on my way to London, so Ray wrote me a letter of introduction to Vera Lynn and her husband, Harry. Vera was due in Toronto for a television taping, and we arranged that she stay over for an additional two days, to appear in the Greatest British Variety Show. I also signed up Gladys Mills, a very popular honky-tonk piano player. My companion, Junie James, who was a violinist as well as a singer, would also be on the show. The Irish Rovers, who had just come out with the song, "The Unicorn," also agreed to be in the show which was booked for March 17, St. Patrick's Day.

On March 17, Vera Lynn sang to 12,862 people—one of the largest audiences of her entire career. Because of our success, we decided to launch a similar show and take it to Ottawa, London, Winnipeg, Edmonton, Calgary, Vancouver, San Francisco, San Diego an Los Angeles.

The greatest mistake of my financial career.

The shows in Toronto, Ottawa and Vancouver I

would handle myself; for the other cities, I arranged for agents to handle the various aspects of production. The agreement was for them to be paid a flat fee, not a percentage. That was undoubtedly the greatest mistake of my financial career. None of the agents did a good job and the crowds we expected never came. In Vancouver we decided to cut our losses—more than $100,000—and cancel the American tour. The strain of this disaster was emotional as well as financial for Junie and myself. We decided together that it would probably be best for her to return to show business, alone. Meanwhile, I stayed in Toronto and tried to untangle the mess that had come from the Greatest British Variety Show. I had been taught a costly lesson; and I would never again become dependent upon others to promote my own affairs.

Born under the astrological sign of Scorpio, I'm the type of person who, when he gets knocked down, becomes a little stronger when he stands up. I had no other alternative at this point but to go to a few friends who were aware of my circumstances and ask them to advance me monies to make up a bankroll. These friends believed in my system at the casinos; and, over the next four months, I hopped between the casinos in the Caribbean and Europe, finally, winning enough money to pay the debts and start in business again. Even when I did not use it, I knew the system could always be counted on to make money when needed.

My business was now doing well again, but emotionally I was still in limbo. For the last year, a young lady by the name of Jaye Golansky had been working in my organization. I barely knew she existed since I was doing a lot of travelling back and forth to Europe and the Caribbean. My secretary was to marry my accountant, and at the church, waiting for the wedding to begin, I felt a tap on my shoulder. It was Jaye, and she gave me a friendly, "Hi, Boss. How're you doing?" She looked lovely.

The last fifteen years have been the best of my entire life.

My own companion and I went to the reception. When we got there Jaye approached us and said, wickedly, "Oh! I've never had the pleasure of being introduced to your wife." She knew I wasn't married, she knew I had broken up with Junie James, but my date was in the dark. "You didn't tell me you were married," she protested, and before I could deny anything, she had disappeared into a crowd of eligible bachelors.

Jaye's remark when I asked for an explanation? "Well, I didn't think she was the right type for you, anyway." The next day, Sunday, I drove to my office, located Jaye's address and went to her home. Would she like to take in a movie? Yes she would, and as we crossed busy Bloor Street on our way to the cinema, Jaye looked up at me and said, nonchalantly, "I'm going to marry you one day." I smiled briefly. A year later another wedding took place — ours. And the last fifteen years have been the best of my entire life.

CHAPTER 16

Our first trip together

When Jaye had come to work for us, her job had been to visit major corporations and discuss with them the advantages of the travel packages we were handling. After our engagement, she concentrated on the Bahamas packages that we put together. She arranged poolside shows, golf tournaments, tours, and whatever else it takes to keep a group of fifty vacationers content. Our travellers were not pupils of the Midas Method, nor were these trips gambling junkets. Simply, a group travelling to the Bahamas for a five-day vacation would retain our services to teach them how not to lose money while gambling. These were always fun trips—especially for the two of us.

The first night Jaye watched me play at the tables remains clear in my mind. I was playing with a $5,000 bankroll, and Jaye would walk by the table from time to time. Sometimes the money was lost, sometimes it was won, but always there was an expression of disbelief on her face. Here was the equivalent of her paycheck being bet; there, a new dress; and there, rent for her apartment.

We were in the Bahamas a couple of days when we decided to rent a motor scooter. I was carrying about $3,000 in cash, in a little change purse, which I asked Jaye to hold for me. After driving for about an hour, we decided to stop for a bite.

An expression of horror covered Jaye's face when she reached into her pocket, and she didn't have to tell me that the change purse was gone. Back and forth along our route we went, looking at the side of the road and in ditches. After a fruitless afternoon there was only one course left to take: win back the full amount that evening — not only for the sake of our bank account, but also to help make Jaye feel a little better than she was feeling that afternoon.

Lady Luck was with me, because it took a mere twenty-five minutes to win back the lost money. The new expression on Jaye's face would have lit up a thousand Christmas trees, and from that evening on, I don't think Jaye has ever worried that we wouldn't recover from a bad financial experience.

You never know who's keeping an eye on you.

There was another casino crisis for Jaye on this trip. A novice still, Jaye was concentrating on the slot machines. She ran out of funds one evening, and seeing me preoccupied at the dice table reached out and helped herself to a few chips from the tray in front of me. No sooner did she walk three feet from the table, than two security guards took her by the arms and brought her back to me, tapped me on my shoulder and asked if I knew her. The lesson here is obvious—you never know who's keeping an eye on you.

CHAPTER 17

Married new year's eve and a three and a half month honeymoon

Jaye and I had worked extremely hard over the last year from the time we had first met, carrying on with our casino evenings for various corporations and charities, assisting in teaching people my Midas Method, and looking after other ventures. On December 31 we flew down to the Bahamas and were married. Then, because we couldn't find a place to stay, we caught an evening flight to New York.

After three days in New York, we came back to Toronto to carry on with our business. I had been teaching Jaye how to play the Midas Method strategy over the last year, and in March I felt it was a good time to take an extended honeymoon. We left for Europe to play for three months. The trip would be an opportunity for Jaye to see some of the world, and to learn, under combat conditions, how to play in the casinos. She would see how the casinos react to a consistent winner, and we would learn all about controlling your emotions at the tables. She had become an exceptionally good pupil, and we took off on the first leg of our journey flying from Toronto to London.

We spent the first week at the Londonderry Hotel on Park Lane. At first, Jaye approached casino life very cautiously. She kept trying to put out the next bet before having pulled in the first bet and not knowing whether the money she had out was the money she had won or the money she should pull back. I'm sure the first session was a very grinding experience for her.

I started her off with a bankroll of £1,000 and she would play to make £100 an evening, or 10%. She did not go up to the table and attempt to reach her quota in one sequence, because she was not conditioned to putting out £50 to £300 in one bet. What she would do was play ten £10 sequences, in which she was only betting relatively small amounts of money — £3, £4, £5 and, at the very most, perhaps £30, at any given time.

I do not work with a compounded bankroll.

There are two ways that you can play in the casino, and a lot of people believe that if you walk in with £1,000 and you win £100, the next night you go in with £1,100 and you win £110, and so forth. Yes, you can do that. However, I have always played with the idea that if I have a £1,000 bankroll and I play to make 10%, when I make the £100 — my profit — I do *not* add it to my bankroll. I put that money aside and I use it to pay for my expenses.

I have never taken my winnings and added it to the total; I do not work with a compounded bankroll. Because that is the way I played that was the way I taught Jaye. I explained to her that she needn't make her 10% in one casino. She might complete one or two sequences in one casino and be halfway through another sequence, get up, leave, and go to another casino. While she was playing her £10 sequences, I, in turn, with a £3,000 bankroll was playing to make a £300 sequence. There were many times at the roulette wheel when the dealers would be changed every few minutes; when one dealer would spin the wheel faster than another; when one would carry on a conversation while the other would be perfectly mute; when one would be gruff and nasty while the other would be pleasant. These were all little psychological touches that could affect a player, and I was happy that Jaye was experiencing the casino environment. I'm sure the first two nights that she played were the most nerve-wracking for her. After our first week in London, Jaye had become quite conditioned to casino life and had won approximately £780 playing at the tables. She played mostly at the roulette wheel; it was a choice of either red or black, odd or even. The win and loss factor is determined very quickly unless, of course, there are a lot of people playing at the table. If that's the case, the game is slowed down a little bit. In blackjack, on the other hand, you have to know the game and know how to draw cards and apply the money management strategy.

My total profit for my week in London was £2,622, and with that in hand we flew to Paris.

There is no gambling in Paris itself, so we rented a car and drove from the city of Enjienne on the capital's outskirts. Jaye would be playing 50 franc sequences, I would play 1,500 franc sequences.

With a bankroll of 5,000 francs, Jaye was playing to make 500 francs in an evening. When we arrived in Enjienne we had dinner and then proceeded to play at the table. After four hours, during which we both played at the roulette wheel—sometimes together, sometimes at different tables—Jaye cashed out 653 francs and I cashed out 3,440. The reason Jaye had made a little more than her objective was that there were a couple of times when she had bet more than she should have, and had won. The language factor was the problem here. Jaye didn't know all the French terminology used by other players. After spending three days in Paris and playing in Enjienne each night, we decided that we would fly to Nice and visit the French Riviera. Using the Negresco Hotel in Nice as our base, we would rent a car and drive to Monte Carlo, which is only a few miles away, or to Cannes, fifty miles away. Some evenings, we would just visit the three casinos in Nice itself.

The trick in being a consistent winner is having enough common sense and discipline to leave when you're ahead.

Our stay in Nice was for two weeks, and while the days were full, the evenings were often boring. We would get dressed up, go to the casinos, walk in with our objective in mind, reach that objective in perhaps half an hour and then leave. Many evenings were spent reading, back at the hotel. Yes, we could have gone to another casino, but one of the most important things in playing the system successfully is this: you set a goal, you remember that goal, and if you accomplish it in a very short period of time, that's fine. Some evenings, you may spend three hours at the tables, because you run into a difficult situation. But once you reach the pre-determined number of sequences, you leave. Why stay any longer? The trick in being a consistent winner is having enough common sense and discipline to leave when you're ahead.

After spending two weeks in Nice, we decided to rent a car and drive on through Italy. We spent the first evening at the casino in San Remo, which is considered the Italian Riviera. Our next stop was just outside Florence, at the improbably named California Motel. The next morning, we decided to exchange our French money and a good portion of our British money into Italian currency. When the bank clerk realized the amount of cash we were exchanging, she immediately ushered us into the office of the manager, who personally conducted the transaction and became so interested in our story that he immediately invited us out for dinner the following evening. After spending three days in Florence with our new-found friends, we headed for Venice and the Island of Lido, with its splendid casino. We stayed at a tiny motel in Lido, and for the week we were there, travelled everywhere by boat.

The gambling in the Lido casino, as in the rest of Europe, is much different from the gambling in Las Vegas or Atlantic City. In Europe, it is all very quiet, very sophisticated, very elegant. Guests are perfectly attired and groomed. The atmosphere is so subdued that, even if there are a thousand people in the casino, you can hear the balls spinning in the roulette wheels. In the cocktail lounge later, Jaye and I met a couple from Hawaii. The husband was a pediatrician, and they were in Venice for a medical convention. In three days they would be going to Nice, to spend a week before returning home. They had seen Jaye play at the roulette table, and they were impressed.

Jaye told them a little about me and our present trip, and we spent the next two hours sitting in the cocktail lounge chatting about gambling, a completely new topic for the doctor and his wife. Yes, I explained, it was possible to win in the casino. And yes, it was possible that I could take an individual, win money for him, and teach him how to win money as well. By this time our bar bill was about 6,000 lire. To prove my point, I took the doctor to the baccarat table, and I made exactly the amount of the money needed. Before the end of the evening, we were all friends and agreed to meet in Nice.

Jaye and I spent another day in Venice, then flew to Frankfurt, Germany, to play in the casinos of that city and those of Weisbaden. Having met our daily objectives, we then flew to Nice. At the Negresco Hotel, we were pleased to learn that our friends from Hawaii were staying there as well. We called them, met in the cocktail lounge, and made plans to spend the next few days visiting the casinos. At the Municipal Casino, where we all had to produce our passports at the door, I began to show the doctor how to apply the strategy. After dinner, he was eager to win enough to cover our tab. As I stood beside him at the roulette wheel I watched him play the various combinations of red-black, odd-even and high and low. Using his own bankroll, he won enough to cover the tab.

You'd better get the hell out of here.

When we all returned to the table, Jaye informed me that a gentleman at the roulette table was picking up her money — it had happened five times. If she had bet on red and red came up, the casino paid her, but the man reached over and picked up the francs. I insisted that we get to the bottom of this nasty situation. Jaye spotted the man at another roulette table and we walked over. A middle-aged woman had just put a bet down on the second dozen, and the number 17 came up. The casino paid her off at 2 to 1, and while another player was being paid off we watched in near disbelief as Mr. Grab reached across the table and picked up the woman's chips. The woman placed another bet, this time on the second dozen — numbers 13 through 24 — and 20 came up on the wheel. When the fellow reached over and picked up the chips and the woman hedged, I realized that she didn't really understand if she was winning or losing; she just assumed she was losing because the money wasn't there when she looked for it. I now waited for the woman to place another bet, which she did on the third dozen. Number 27 came up. The casino girl paid her off at 2 to 1, and immediately the long-armed fellow reached out for her chips. Quietly, I put my hand out right across the table, grabbed him by the wrist, and looked him straight in the eye. "That's enough," I said. "You'd better get the hell out of here." The fellow walked to the door and out the casino.

The lesson here? Always be aware of how much money you place down, and how much you have won. Don't take things for granted. There are people who do little else but visit the gambling casinos and look for players who are not quite sure of what they are doing. The chips have no initials on them, no name on them. If there's ever an argument, most witnesses will say nothing — they don't want to be embarrassed in case they've made a mistake by accusing the wrong individual. The chap who picks up the money has practically everything going for him.

After a few drinks, the doctor decided to return to the roulette table. He won enough to pay the bar bill and then we went on to another casino. Here, the doctor, his wife and Jaye decided that they would just watch for a while. About fifteen minutes later the pit-boss came over to me and asked if I had had dinner. If not, would I be a guest of the casino? Where was I staying? How long would I be in town? At that particular time I had won four of the six bets I had placed, so I wasn't doing anything extraordinary. Whether or not he felt that I was a different type of player, I really don't know. Considering the short period we had been in the casino, his generosity was quite overwhelming.

After I placed a few more bets we returned to the Negresco for a cocktail before retiring. The following day, we decided we would visit the Island of Corsica. A boat left from Nice at six in the monring, and the crossing took six hours.

At 4:30 AM we were the only people on the promenade in Nice, singing and dancing our way toward the boat dock. The crossing was delightful, and when we arrived in Corsica around noon, we rented a car and drove down the west side of the island.

Corsica, we soon discovered, is a wine-taster's haven. At the first winery we visited, our tour was capped off with four samples. We also picked up some bottles of our favourite vino, then on to the next winery for some more, then to the next one and then to the next. Need I say more than I don't remember very much of the Island of Corsica, but I do know that we all had a smashing time.

When we arrived back in Nice, we went on to Cannes. In a matter of hours at the tables we covered our Corsica expenses.

Our friends returned to Hawaii a few days later, and Jaye and I spent the next two weeks on the Riviera. Then we had a week in Paris, on to London, and back home. After three and a half months of a beautiful honeymoon, gambling almost every night and winning consistently, we were back in Toronto — completely exhausted, but happy.

CHAPTER 18

School for gamblers

We were back in Toronto, and now it was time for me to settle down and concentrate on my business. We were becoming more involved in renting gambling equipment, and charities were now becoming interested in using our services as a way to raise funds. At that time, the government was issuing licences to charities, allowing individuals to gamble at the tables with a maximum $1 bet per hand. This seemed to be quite a successful way of raising money for charity. Everyone loves to gamble, and the $1 ceiling kept the charities from losing money. We became quite busy helping various groups.

Meanwhile, we decided to branch out by setting up a gaming school in Toronto. We would teach individuals how to play the various casino games intelligently. On checking with my lawyer about operating such a school, I was told that it was quite legal so long as we were not playing with real money, and that my games were being used for the purpose of instruction only.

An inspector of the Morality Squad advised me that I could be charged—no gaming school would open its doors in the City of Toronto.

The improbable location of our gaming school was above a bagel bakery. When I informed the police department of our setup, the first reaction was that it was an illegal operation. An inspector of the Morality Squad advised me that I could be charged — no gaming school would open its doors in the City of Toronto. I informed the inspector that my lawyer had said such a school was, in fact, quite legal, and that I would open the business as scheduled. I would be only too pleased to explain to him in detail exactly the way the school would be run. We would be every bit as kosher as the bakery below us. Within a half hour the police came over for an inspection tour, and for the first six weeks of operations they made almost daily visits. They would run up the stairs as fast as they could, then rush through the doors in the hope of being able to catch us in the midst of some illegal activity. During this period I offered them an extra room that I had at the school. I was prepared to put in a couch and a television set for them, and if they wished, they could sit there all day and monitor everything that was going on in the school.

My purpose in opening the school had been in response to a need. I had been renting equipment to various organizations to run casino evenings at halls and hotels throughout the city. With our permanent location, handsomely decorated, private corporations could hold a party at a centralized spot. The response proved that there was a real need for such an operation. Guests were able to have practical experience they couldn't find anywhere else unless they went to a casino—and if they went to the casino they would be paying a lot of money for their education. For $10, on the other hand, they could come to our school and learn to play the games intelligently, using non-negotiable chips.

One group to book was the Presidents' and Vice-Presidents' Club in Canada, an organization of executives of American corporations operating companies in Toronto. They arranged in advance for their banquet permit. On the day of the event, however, the club was informed at noon that its liquor permit had been revoked. At this point, we had been operating for eight months — staff had been trained and the wrinkles had been ironed out.

When told of the problem with the licence, three members of the Presidents' Club immediately paid a visit to the Liquor Control Board. No explanation was offered.

There was one solution: cocktails would be served at the home of a club member, a bus would be rented to shuttle guests between our school and the home, and dinner without beverages would be served on our premises. At three in the afternoon, a club member found himself in the novel position of telling his wife to expect 400 guests for dinner. We managed to charter a bus and the evening somehow was successful.

It was back to doing what I did best. Playing the system.

The liquor board was later to explain that the licence had been revoked because it felt that if the people were drinking and gambling at the tables, they wouldn't be happy playing with funny money; the next thing, they would be gambling for real. We were informed that the powers-to-be had no intention of ever issuing a banquet permit to any group who wished to rent our facilities for an evening. This was a severe blow for us. After trying to keep our school afloat without the banquet facility, we were forced to close our doors and returned to our old system of bringing the games to the people and not the reverse.

I had no alternative but to salvage what I could and prepare myself to go back to the casinos. Canada's first gaming school had an impeccable record. The customers were satisfied as well as the police. But without the drinks we could not turn a profit. And so it was back to doing what I did best. Playing the system.

CHAPTER 19

Getting around in London

As the dealer was paying me the £300 I had just won, I quickly checked my money to see if my goal for the evening had been reached. I realized that I had won £2,200 so far, and figured it was a pretty good night's work for four hours at the table, and proceeded to the cashier to turn my chips into currency.

Get him out of here!

Walking through the maze of tables and watching the action still going on, I was not aware of what was going on behind me. When I reached the top of the staircase leading out of the building, I suddenly felt gorilla-like hands on my shoulders, pushing me as quickly as possible down the flight of stairs to the floor below. Someone flung open the casino door and pushed me quickly outside, opened the door of my car and threw me into it while shouting to the driver, "Get him out of here!"

As the car started to pull away from the curb, I saw more policemen than I'd ever seen in my life. There must have been fifty or sixty bobbies standing in the street around the casino. I hadn't an inkling what was going on. Only when I got back to my hotel room, having put my money away in the cashier's cage in the lobby, did my bodyguard come rushing in the door to inform me of what had taken place at the small casino in Soho.

While I had been playing at the dice table in the casino, he had overheard conversations from three or four fellows who were walking around and eyeing my money, which I had placed in front of me at the dice table. It was a Greek club, and my Greek is non-existent, so I was not aware of what was being said about me as I played at the tables. I had been losing for most of the first two hours that I had been playing, and now I had started to win back some of my losses. The majority of people playing at the tables were betting £1 and £5; I was now betting £50, £100 and up—as much as £300 on one bet. Naturally, I attracted a lot of attention. When I walked away from the table, after having won my £300 bet, my bodyguard had overheard three fellows mention that they were going to attack me as I walked down the small staircase leading out of the building.

Luckily, Nick, my bodyguard, understood Greek. When he saw me leaving the cashier's cage, walking toward the staircase, he immediately placed his hands on my shoulders and pushed me down the stairs at great speed, out through the door and into my car, then instructed my chauffeur to get me out of there as quickly as possible.

The policemen's appearance, it turned out, was strictly coincidental. My bodyguard was as amazed as I to see all the bobbies standing there. After getting me into the car, Nick went over to one of the policemen to find out what had happened. Apparently, about fifteen minutes before we had left the building, someone had attempted to rob one of the downstairs lounges. The police had been called and the suspect had been cornered at the back of one of the buildings. For me, the timing was beautiful. As soon as the threesome caught sight of the bobbies, they took flight in different directions, losing me completely.

When I first started travelling to London, I really did not know the places to go to or the places to stay away from. The smart thing to do, I was told, was to hire a chauffeur and tell him my plans for the evening. He, with his expertise, would be able to suggest spots of interest, take me there, and be sure that I avoided the sleazier places — especially if I was carrying large sums of money.

Over the years, my chauffeur and I became quite good friends. Trevor's cousin, David, happened to be with the Flying Squad of the London police department. When Dave had told his colleagues that his cousin was chauffeuring a fellow from Canada who had a system for winning at the casinos, you can imagine their skepticism. So on one of my trips, Dave asked if I would be prepared to chat with his policeman friends.

I spent four hours with the chaps from the flying squad, telling them about my experiences over the years in various casinos and about my system that won consistently. We then made arrangements for the group to meet Trevor and myself at my hotel at 9:30. We would visit the various casinos in London, and I would prove to them that my system worked successfully. First we went to the Mayfair Club, which is in Berkley Square; then to the Curzon House; then to Les Ambassadors. From there we went to the Victoria Sporting Club and finally, at four o'clock in the morning, we ended up back in Berkley Square, at the Colony Club, where George Raft was the greeter. I had met Mr. Raft many times previously, and as we entered the club he escorted our group over to one of the dice tables and made room for me to play. I played at the table for half an hour and I won about £700. I then invited all my guests for a mid-morning breakfast of steak and champagne, and after we had finished the meal, I requested the cheque from the waiter. Mr. Raft came over to the table and politely informed us that the steak and champagne were compliments of the house. My guests were now believers that my system worked successfully.

On leaving the casino I went to the dice table and played to make an additional £100 — in a matter of three minutes. Then I had the four £25 chips drilled by the casino, and gave one to each of the four gentlemen from the flying squad, to attach to their keychains.

As the evening had been so successful, my guests offered me the services of an off-duty policeman whenever I requested one. I would pay this bodyguard his fee for the evening simply to follow me around from casino to casino, not necessarily standing beside me but keeping his watchful eye on everything that happened around me. In many instances, I did not know who the bodyguard was on a given evening. He could have been the man standing beside me at one of the gaming tables, or drinking with me at the bar. Or he could have just been walking around the casino as a spectator. His purpose was to protect me and my money until I got safely back to the hotel.

CHAPTER 20

Barred in England

Casinos do not like consistent winners. With my strategy I am in and out of a casino in about twenty minutes. I set a goal each evening, an amount I want to win that is in proportion to the bankroll I am carrying. Let us assume that I am carrying £2,000. With a bankroll of that size, I would play to make ten to fifteen percent profit in an evening—£200 to £300. I would not, however, attempt to make £200 or £300 each time I walked into a casino. If that were the case, if I went into ten casinos in an evening I would make ten times my ten to fifteen percent objective. At that rate I could very easily double my bankroll each night. But I am careful—extremely careful—to resist this temptation. Sooner or later, the casinos would become very upset and refuse me the chance to play again. Discretion and a low profile are all important if you want to avoid being barred! If it happened that after three-quarters of an hour I had only won £100, I would leave the casino. Whatever else I needed to win to achieve my goal, I would probably pick up at the next casino we visited.

The more you play my strategy, the more confidence you build within yourself, knowing that you'll win your objective. Sure, there may be times when you become involved in a long sequence where the wheel goes against you, or the cards go against you, or the dice go against you. You may have many more losses than you have wins. But by knowing *how* to bet your money and not deviating from your plan, you will pull yourself out and show a profit.

If you can win all the time, why don't you go in and break the bank?

It's very difficult to get people to believe that you really can walk into a casino and meet your objective. Their immediate reaction is, if you can win all the time, why don't you go in and break the bank? First of all, the casinos quite simply are not going to allow that to happen. If you go into a casino and you win consistently, £100 a night, that's fine: they may tolerate you. But they are going to be aware of what you're doing, they are going to know that you are a different kind of player. They know you don't deviate, you don't get confused, you don't get angry and you don't get greedy — and that is a difficult combination to beat. So, aware that management knows that you are a winner, why *should* you go into the casino with the attitude that you're going to strike it rich? Remember — always remember — that if you start taking them for a tremendous amount of money, they're going to end up barring you.

The key is to remember that every casino is a bank. You can walk in and withdraw amounts in proportion to your bankroll.

Eventually, if you play for years in a given town, you suddenly realize that you're playing on borrowed time. The casino management can come up to you at any time and prevent you from placing any more bets at the table. They do not want consistent winners. My method, therefore, is to hit and run. Walk in, make small amounts of money, and try not to upset the casino. In fact, in a lot of cases, I have walked out of a casino when I was involved in a long sequence—not because the system didn't work, but because I wanted the casino to feel that it had the opportunity of winning back some of its money — and welcome me back the following day. There are many tricks that a serious player of the system will acquire in order to remain a welcome, or relatively unnoticed, guest. Once again, the key is to remember that every casino is a bank. You can walk in and withdraw amounts in proportion to your bankroll. The opportunity won't go away — so long as you are psychologically prepared to get involved in a long sequence — a sequence where you are experiencing more losses than wins. Eventually, if you stick with it you'll pull it off, tempting though it may be to say to yourself, "Enough!" You never know when you may run into the long sequence.

Casinos love system players. Their attitude is that the system player is not really different from any other player—he just loses his money more systematically.

For every person who is conditioned to apply a strategy for winning money, there are hundreds who are capable of learning the strategy but not of applying it — they do not have the guts or the psychological temperament required to keep on playing in the face of severe losses. It's a matter of walking into the casino, setting a predetermined goal, playing till you make that amount of money, and then taking a break. Normally, you can meet your objective, irrespective of the amount of money played, in from twenty seconds to twenty minutes.

Casinos love system players. Their attitude is that the system player is not really different from any other player—he just loses his money more systematically. If a person shows a little more expertise in playing than the average gambler, the casino is not likely to be perturbed. But there are occasions when casinos do get upset.

Casinos get upset for a number of reasons. To put it coldly, casinos bar consistent winners or card counters because they regard those players as a disease — and they want to keep the disease from spreading.

On one of my trips to London I took five friends with me. Over a period of two weeks they came to my hotel room in the daytime, where I taught them the system. One evening, they walked into a casino and started to play the roulette wheel. Each person was playing with a different objective in mind; one was playing red and black, one odd and even, and two high and low. After they played for about an hour, with each one consistently winning, the pit-boss walked over to the group and, pointing to the other roulette table, said "That's the table for children; this is the table for adults. Why don't you move over to the children's table?" Now you can imagine their feelings of embarrassment in a casino in front of complete strangers. Their first reaction was anger. Then there was confusion — what amount of money had they placed? had red or black just come up on the wheel? odd or even? low or high? The players left the table and the casino was smiling. Mission accomplished. As it turned out, after a drink to calm our nerves, we went to another casino and picked up where we had left off — meeting our objectives.

I have been barred from the Curzon House, the Knightsbridge, the Olympia Casino, the Mayfair Club, and, when the Mayfair's owners took over its management, George Raft's Colony Club.

The general public does not clearly understand that a casino can bar you. They do not understand that these multi-million dollar corporations, and even the small casinos in some countries, will bar you not for the amount of money that you win from them, but because you do it continually.

Take the case of Hughie Green, a Canadian living in England who during the years 1965 through 1973 was host of the popular program, "Sky's the Limit," which aired to millions of people each Friday night. A mutual friend suggested that he could get me on the show, and he introduced me to Hughie Green. Mr. Green was intrigued by my Midas Touch and agreed to put me on as a contestant.

When you appear on "Sky's the Limit," you select questions from various categories and, by answering them correctly, can win up to £100. The show takes place before a live audience. Luck was with me and I won my bundle of 100 single pound notes. Handing me my winnings, Hughie Green said, "Well, Mr. Irwin, I guess you are now going to go to the casinos."

"That's right, Mr. Green," I replied. "I *am* going to go to the casinos. But I would now like to challenge any newspaperman in England to go with me to a casino of his choice. I will take my £100 and whatever I make I will donate to the reporter's favourite charity."

He was a skeptic and certainly did not believe that there was such a thing as a system.

Mr. Green announced to all of Britain, "Well, there you go, gentlemen, there's an opportunity. Mr. Irwin has offered a challenge and we would like to have him come back next week and tell us what has transpired. For any reporters out there listening who would like to write to me personally, I will set up a meeting with Mr. Irwin and we'll have you both back here next week." With that I took the £100 and made my exit. Two days later, Hughie Green called me at my hotel to tell me that one of the top columnists of the *Daily Mirror* had accepted the challenge. Would I meet him that evening at my hotel?

At 6:30 that night, Clifford Davis met with me in the cocktail lounge of the Londonderry Hotel. He was not a gambler, he told me. In fact, he was a skeptic and certainly did not believe that there was such a thing as a system. He accepted my challenge and wanted me to prove to him that I could in fact take the £100 and go to a casino and make money. We would go to the Playboy Club first.

When we entered the club we went to the top floor, and as we walked in the hostess took us over to my favourite table. We ordered a drink, and soon Mr. Davis was telling my companion how beautiful she looked that evening. She remarked that she had just spent £55 for the new dress she was wearing for the occasion.

"Could you really do that anytime you want, at any casino I want?"

That was my cue, and without a second's hesitation I took her by the hand, telling Clifford to remain seated, and walked with her into the gaming area. Which game did she like the best, I asked. She wasn't sure, but seeing we were standing at the roulette wheel, she said "Let's try this one." I immediately put down some money on the table and within three minutes I won the £55 and presented them to her. Back at the table in the dining area, she was obviously very enthusiastic. After she explained to Clifford what I had done, she laughed that she was only sorry that she hadn't told us she had spent £15 getting her hair done for the occasion. So I swept her to the craps table and within twenty-five seconds won her the £15. You can imagine Clifford's surprise — in a few minutes we had won £70. Over dinner the reporter kept asking me "Could you really do that anytime you want, at any casino I want?"

The bill for dinner was £35. After dessert I took Clifford to the craps table, showed him how I played my strategy, and within three minutes won the cost of our dinner. It was now time to play the £100 won on "Sky's the Limit."

Playing to make £10 sequences, we tried the roulette, blackjack and craps tables. Clifford said that he couldn't understand why I was barred from a casino. In his mind, there was no casino that could bar me. I told him that I was barred from the Park Lane casino, which was just around the corner from the Playboy Club, and he expressed disbelief. There was only one way to convince him, so I suggested we walk around the corner and see what would happen. As we entered the front foyer of the Park Lane Casino, the doorman motioned to the concierge at the desk that I was coming in. I asked him if my membership was going to be reinstated, following my recent written application, and he informed me that no decision had been made. The casino manager was out, the assistant manager was out, and his assistant was also out. Meanwhile, Clifford was becoming very upset and politely asked the concierge why I was barred from the club in the first place. The reply was that the casino does not want a consistent winner; Mr. Irwin wins consistently, therefore the casino does not want him and so his membership had been revoked. Clifford informed the man that he was a member of the press, and that this story should be related in the newspapers, making the general public aware what was happening to Bruce Irwin. Clifford was no longer a skeptic. With my chauffeur we visited five other casinos in London, ending the session at six in the morning. I had paid for our dinner, all our drinks, a dress and a hairdo. And, from the same £100 bankroll I had made an additional £170, which I turned over to Clifford Davis to hold in safe keeping until we appeared on "Sky's the Limit."

On Friday night, Clifford and I appeared on "Sky's the Limit," and the columnist explained to a listening audience of thirty million people what I had done in the casino — how I had played at the tables, how I had turned £100 into an additional £170 plus the cost of dinner and drinks, how he had visited a casino that barred me because I was a consistent winner. It was then announced that the winnings would be donated to the Al Koran Fund, in aid of the British magician, who was seriously ill in America.

Since that time, Clifford has assisted me in running correspondence courses and teaching people in England how to win at the casinos using the Midas Method. Meanwhile, the London clubs that barred me have either lost their licence or gone out of business. Needless to say, I was never allowed to renew my membership in any of those clubs. At the moment, however, I am welcome in every club in the city.

Casinos do not like a consistent winner. It is not the amount of money you win in the casino at one time that upsets them, it is the manner in which you win it. If you were to walk into the casino and win $10,000 in an evening, the management would cater to you and treat you like a king. But if you were to play in that same casino for a period of a week, and only win $100 an evening and do it consistently, that's going to upset the folks upstairs. The large amount of money in one night shows them that you've just been lucky. The reason they'll cater to you is because they want you to continue playing in that casino—so that the house can win back its money. But by playing consistently and winning consistently night after night for a period of a week, no matter how little you win, they know that you are an intelligent player. You do not deviate. You do not get confused. You do not get angry. And, above all, you're not greedy. And that is a very tough combination for any casino to beat!

The Board of Directors had had a meeting and had decided to revoke my membership.

On my visits to London, I often stay at the

Londonderry Hotel on Park Lane. One morning while staying there a letter was waiting for me in my mailbox at the front desk, from the Curzon House. The Board of Directors, it stated, had had a meeting and had decided to revoke my membership. Therefore, I was no longer permitted to play in that club. When I went personally to the Curzon House to find out the board's objections, I was treated by everyone there as if I had suddenly picked up some highly contagious disease. No one would give me any information about why I was rejected by the club. Not a hint of an explanation.

Four days later I received a similar letter from the Park Lane casino. Once again, no reasonable explanation was given as to why I was barred. One staffer commented that I was a consistent winner, and they did not want consistent winners. During the period from 1970 through 1973, I was barred from six casinos in London because of my winning consistently at the tables. First I was barred from the Curzon House, then the Park Lane casino, the Mayfair casino, the Knightsbridge casino, the Olympic casino, and the Pair of Shoes casino.

The casinos in Europe, especially in London, operate differently from the casinos in Las Vegas, Atlantic City or the Caribbean. In Las Vegas and Atlantic City almost anyone can enter the casino and play. In the Caribbean, permanent residents cannot play the casinos. The European casinos are generally private clubs, although under the jurisdiction of the respective country's gaming board. In London, you must make an application to become a member of a club at least forty-eight hours before being granted permission to play. One of the reasons behind this regulation is that a person should not be "enticed" into the gambling casino.

The simple truth is that casinos—anywhere— do not like consistent winners.

A few years ago, some London clubs had entertainment facilities directly connected with the casino portion; they were made to change their setup, requiring a separate entrance for the casino and a separate entrance for the entertainment section.

Because they are private clubs, the casinos in England have the opportunity of revoking your membership at their own discretion, without giving any reason. And ninety-five percent of the people barred just walk away from the place and don't do anything about it. The simple truth is that casinos — anywhere — do not like consistent winners. They will use any means to get rid of any individual who, they feel, is going to be detrimental to the success of their operation.

One evening when I returned to my hotel, my chauffeur suggested that I had never been to a casino called the Pair of Shoes, which was located directly behind the Londonderry Hotel. So I said, "Well, let's go in and see if we can make some money." He parked the car and joined me and we walked into the casino. After I produced cards that showed I was a member of other casinos, the attendants allowed me upstairs into the gaming area which, at the time, had one dice table, one baccarat table, four blackjack tables, and one roulette table. That was it. In the casinos in London, you don't have the opportunity of drinking at the tables as you do in Nevada and Atlantic City. If you're going to do any drinking, you do it in another room, quite apart from the casino area.

Having had a drink when we first walked into the Pair of Shoes, I ventured over to the dice table. After playing for about forty minutes, I had won £1,055. I then walked over to the cashier to change the chips into currency, and spent the next forty-five minutes waiting for the exchange to be completed. Eventually, the manager came over to me and offered a cheque, which I promptly refused. In London, you don't accept a cheque from a casino if you're planning to visit another house—one casino will not cash another's cheques. So I refused the cheque, and held onto the chips for three days, at which point the Pair of Shoes was in a financial position to pay me off. It was my understanding, from one of the employees in the casino, that the casino's bankroll was £35! Not surprisingly, the Pair of Shoes is no longer in business, and many of the other smaller casinos that I used to frequent have closed their doors as well.

CHAPTER 21

Interesting escapades

St. Marten

One evening in the late 1970's, I received a call from a friend inviting me to join a group going to St. Marten for a weekend of gambling. There were nine of us in the group from Toronto, I would say that basically everybody was more or less a high-roller, and we joined the rest of the group in New York.

After arriving in St. Marten and having spent a few days there relaxing in the sun and playing in the casinos in the evening, we were to leave for Toronto on a Sunday. At that point we were all winners from the casino, the least amount won was $700.

As we were sitting around the pool on the Sunday morning having breakfast and talking about our experiences over the last four days, we were informed by the casino manager that the plane that was to take us back in the afternoon had blown a tire when it had landed in Jamaica that morning and because they had to fly another wheel down from Toronto, we were going to be staying overnight at the hotel and flying back on the Monday.

About an hour later the casino manager informed us that the casino was normally closed on a Sunday evening but because there was nothing else for us to do and we were more or less locked in overnight, they decided to open the casino at 9:00 PM to give us a chance to have some action.

During the afternoon while we were sunning and enjoying ourselves with refreshments, we decided that we would all go to the casino that night and each one of us would take no more than $500, and as the lowest amount of winnings was $700 we felt that even if we all went to the casino that evening and lost $500 each, everyone would still come back a winner.

After a delightful dinner in the dining room of the hotel we all proceeded into the gaming room. One of the chaps who was a blackjack player went to the blackjack table while the rest of us proceeded to the dice table. We all bought $500 worth of chips and proceeded to play.

After about two hours of playing the table was running hot and cold and I would say that each one of us was probably down anywhere from $200 to $300 of our original $500 stake. All of a sudden the chap next to me said, "I think it's time that we turned this table around" and with that picked up the dice and started to roll, and continued to roll for the next twenty-five minutes making nothing but passes and points. The dice then came to me and I continued on for fifteen or twenty minutes with a strong roll, and by 11:40 PM that particular evening, the eight of us had hit that particular table for $146,000. I remember one chap by the name of Donnie who said that when he had $50,000 he was going to quit. He had about $46,000 in racks in front of him, an $1,800 laydown on the dice table and about another $4,000 in his hand. Unfortunately, before we could get him away from the table, he dropped $24,000 chasing the $1,800 laydown that he lost. However, we walked away successfully, having won that

$146,000. The casino was so upset that they called Aruba the following morning and had the tabletop changed to the Aruba craps tabletop which meant that there was no Come or Don't Come on the craps table and that was really the reason that we made as much money as we did because we were not only playing the Pass Line and taking the odds, but we were also playing the Come on every throw of the dice and everybody for a period of well over an hour was doing nothing else but making points and making numbers continually. The casino finally closed at 11:45 PM and the next morning at 7:00 AM we all lined up at the cashier's cage and were paid off in bundles of $1,000 in $20 bills all placed in little brown paper bags.

Needless to say, the casino continued to send each one of us telegrams once and twice a week for the next two or three weeks inviting us to come back at their expense for another round at the tables. It is my understanding to this day that no one accepted their offer.

Atlantic City.

I remember one night in the casino in Atlantic City. I'm basically a black chip player, however I do play with green chips, but this particular night I had been playing with both black and green chips, and I had cashed $500 at the blackjack table and subsequently lost the $500. I cashed another $500 and lost that. I cashed another $500 and was still getting an extremely bad run of cards, so I got up from that table and walked over to the next table. After sitting down at the second blackjack table I proceeded to cash another $500 chip which in a matter of about fifteen or twenty minutes, I also lost, so I cashed another $500 worth of chips and within a few minutes the cards seemed to turn in my favor.

I was getting exceptionally good hands, previous to that, for the last hour, I had been getting stiff hands (hands where you have a 14, 15 or a 12 against the dealer's 17 or 20 or 19) and now I started getting hands where I had 18, 19, 20's and 21's. Eventually after playing for about twenty-five or thirty minutes I had run the amount of money up to about $5,000, which taking into consideration my losses at the previous table and the money I had cashed at this table, meant I was still up about $2,500.

I then asked the pit-boss if I could buy back the $500 chips that I had cashed in at the other table which he permitted me to do, but because they didn't have any $500 chips at that particular table I was playing at, he suggested that I take all the $100 chips that I had and go to the next table, as that dealer had a row of $500 chips. I had decided that I was finished playing and got up from the table putting all the chips into my pocket and walking over to the second table to change the color from black to purple. As I walked up to the blackjack table there were three empty spots in the middle of the table with two players on either side playing the other four boxes. It was my intention to take the $100 chips that I had and get them converted to $500 chips. As I proceeded to pull them out of my pocket and lay them on the table in front of me I suddenly decided that I would make a bet at each one of the empty boxes and immediately placed $500 on the three boxes in front of me. To the first hand I got a pair of 2's, to the second hand a pair of 3's, to the third hand a pair of 4's. The dealer had a 4 showing. After the dealer played the first two hands to my right I decided to split the two 2's and placed another $500 bet. To the first deuce I received a 7 which is a double down situation and doubled the bet and drew a 10. To the second deuce I drew an 8 another double down situation and drew a 9. Splitting my pair of 3's I drew a 7 to the first 3 — doubled that down and drew an Ace. To the second 7 I drew a 2 — doubled that bet and drew an Ace. Splitting the 4's I drew a 5 to that first 4 for a double down and drew a 10. To the other 4 I drew a 7 — doubled it down and drew a 10. The dealer proceeded to play the other two hands and in turning over her hole card — she had a 9 in the hole to give her a 13 — drew a 2 for a 15 — drew another 9 for a 24 and went bust. My $500 bet on the first three positions that I was playing, with all my double downs, ended up being worth $6,000. At that point I then changed all the $100 chips into $500 chips, walked away from the table, cashed in and came home.

CHAPTER 22

Barred in Atlantic City

It is difficult for most people to believe that casinos can bar you at their discretion, without any reasonable explanation. This happened to me again just recently, in Atlantic City in August 1981.

At that time, I had visited almost 1,500 gambling casinos throughout the world, and people were asking me what I thought of Atlantic City. At that point, there were only a couple of casinos operating. I hadn't been there yet because I had heard that it was quite crowded, and you had to wait a long time in order to get a seat at a table. Once you got a seat, if the cards weren't running right and you wanted to get up and leave, you might reconsider because it could take three or four hours before you got another seat.

My wife and I decided to go to Atlantic City, asked our friends, Mr. and Mrs. Charlie Coleman to join us, and made reservations for one night at Harrah's Hotel. After checking into the hotel and getting organized in our rooms, we proceeded to go downstairs to the casino area.

When I walk into any casino, I become a totally different person.

Now my wife, who has been with me on countless trips to the casinos, is fully aware that when

I walk into a casino, I become a totally different person. Gambling to me is an emotionless business, and one must be prepared in a casino to function like a machine. It is only natural that when I walk into a casino, my wife goes her way and I go mine. To prevent drawing any additional attention to myself, I have always made a point of being dressed in the same style as most of the other players and by being very casual. I proceeded up to the blackjack table, sat down and bought $1,000 worth of chips. I played at the table for approximately one hour, and during that period, the dealer was extremely hot. Of the hundred hands that I was dealt during that hour, I lost eighty-two. Yet I still had a profit of $185 when the security man came up and tapped me on the shoulder, flashed his badge in front of me, and requested that I step away from the table; he wanted to speak with me. Had he stopped me two minutes earlier, I would have had a profit of $250; however, I had just lost a bet of $65. When I stepped away from the table, he informed me that the casino had instructed him to inform me that I was barred from playing at the blackjack table, because I was too strong a player, and a card counter. I immediately grabbed him by the right hand and shook it, and thanked him for barring me. I informed him that I was not a card counter but that I had written books on gambling and was also a consultant on gambling. I was in the process of writing a new book and as I had not been barred from a casino for eight years, I was grateful because I now had a current casino barring me. He immediately took three steps backwards and did not say one other thing. I followed him to the security desk, asking if I could meet with the casino manager. It was as if I didn't even exist. At no time would he give me any further information or help.

When I walked back into the area where I had been playing at the table, my friend Charlie said that if I had come back to Toronto and told him that I had been barred from this multi-million-dollar establishment because I had won $185 at the table, he would have suggested that I had lost my marbles. However, he had been there all the time. He had stood behind the table for the hour that I had played; he had seen each and every hand that I had played; and he was prepared to write the testimonial for my new book if and when I asked him to do so.

It is not the amount of money that you win; it's the manner in which you play the game and win the money.

What upset the casino the most was the fact that even though the dealer was having a hot hand, and all the other players at the table had changed two or three times, I was still able to hold my own and still show a profit. Their concern was that, should the cards take a turn for the better for me, I could win a lot of money. Therefore, they simply barred me from playing at the table.

I then walked over to the table at which my wife was playing. At this point, she had won $1,900. Everybody was having fun at the table, laughing, joking, telling stories. The pit-boss was standing there joking and laughing along with them. But the dealer was having an unfortunate run of cards. So, because everyone else at the table was winning, it was only natural that my wife should be winning, too. All of which tells you that it is not the amount of money that you win, it's the manner in which you play the game and win the money.

I returned to Toronto on Sunday evening and the next day phoned Harrah's, requesting to speak to the casino manager. Eventually an assistant to the manager came to the phone. What was my problem? I explained what had happened on Friday evening, and he said that he would look into the situation. If I was prepared to hold he would get right back to me. Twenty minutes later he returned, to inform me that, yes, I had been looked at as a counter of cards, and I had been barred because the house felt that I was doing something out of the ordinary. I informed the gentleman once again that I was not a card counter, and then I proposed a challenge: I would be prepared to write on a slip of paper the amount of money that I was going to win at each game, playing my Mathematical Money Management strategy against the roulette, the blackjack, the craps and the baccarat tables. I would win the designated amount of money in a very short period of time. Hence, I was no card counter, and my system was not specifically for blackjack, but for any casino game. He told me to hold once again, and after another fifteen minutes came back on the line and suggested that I could play the roulette, the craps and the baccarat tables, but not blackjack.

At this point, I suggested that the casino manager could play my cards for me at the table. I would sit on the top floor in the hotel and I would converse by telephone with the manager at the blackjack table. I would permit him to play in whatever manner necessary, depending upon the cards that he drew and the cards that the dealer had. I would only tell him the amount of money that should be bet, depending upon whether he was winning or losing. I would still win whatever predetermined amount of money I had written on the slip of paper and put into a sealed envelope.

After I held the line for another fifteen minutes, he returned to tell me that the casino was not interested, at that point in time, in accepting any challenge. There was a case before the courts at the moment by a chap named Ken Uston, who is a card counter, related to his being barred from playing in the casinos. Uston had taken the case to the New Jersey courts for a ruling, and a decision should be handed down within two weeks' time. Harrah's was going to wait for the decision before making any other arrangements regarding my challenge.

About a month later the New Jersey courts handed down a decision that it was permissible for card counters to play in the casinos; the casinos could not bar them because of their expertise in being able to count the cards. The casinos in Atlantic City immediately appealed the decision to a higher court and in the ruling handed down in June, 1982 the Supreme Court upheld the lower court ruling. Card counters were now permitted to play. On August 1, the card counters were allowed back into the casinos.

As long as two and two make four there is absolutely no way that the casino can beat me —providing the game is not set up or the shoe rigged.

It is my understanding that the casinos have had many discussions among themselves on how to counteract the card counter. In one method, the dealer deals five hands out of a six-deck shoe to each player and then immediately shuffles the cards. For the other, there is a red shoe and a black shoe. Each shoe contains six decks of cards. As the dealer pulls a card out of the red shoe, for example, and if the card happens to be a heart or a diamond, he would proceed to take another card from the red shoe. However, if the card is black, he would then switch over and take one card out of the black shoe. With my particular strategy, it does not matter whether the dealer used forty-seven shoes with forty-seven different colors. I am still going to win money, and as long as two and two make four there is absolutely no way that the casino can beat me—providing the game is not set up or the shoe rigged.

CHAPTER 23

Junkets

Junkets have been around for the last ten years or so. A casino has a representative in a major city who will put together groups of people considered to be high-rollers. By placing either a credit line or up-front money, ranging from $2,000 to $15,000, an individual can fly to a casino in Atlantic City, Las Vegas, the Caribbean or Monte Carlo. The casino pays for airfare and hotel accommodation, and will wine and dine the high-roller while he's gambling. It's certainly not the casino's way of being charitable. Management expects its guests to play at its tables — not do too much wandering while they're in town. Not only is there a moral obligation on the part of the gambler, there's also a financial one. Many casinos will not allow a junket guest to cash any of the chips that he draws in the casino. These chips are placed back into the cage, and the gambling proceeds with receipts and markers. The only time the player actually may see his money again is when he has decided to return home. At this point, whatever profit shows above his line of credit for the cash he placed up front is paid out. If the customer owes money, he issues a check against the line of credit or subtracts the amount from the cash placed up front.

The casinos, you see, have the junket timed perfectly.

I have been on only a few junkets in the last ten

years — I am not that type of player. Being a strategy player, my attitude and my approach are different from those of a gambler. If I walk into a casino with $5,000, that is my bankroll. I'm looking to make ten to fifteen percent of that amount, possibly in one or two sequences. If I were to go on a junket and put the same $5,000 into the cage, then to play my system I would have to go to the table and draw that amount in chips. And if I were to do that—draw the whole amount at one time — the casino would not be so accommodating. The casinos, you see, have the junket timed perfectly. They realize that on the first and second days the player may end up winning money, and on the third and fourth days he loses. They don't need a loser around on the fifth day — so junkets usually run about four days. And by that time, ninety-five percent of the players are cleaned out and the casino is looking for a new junket to come in. The casino cannot make money from losers.

So if I were to draw $5,000 at one time, someone would likely come up and say, "Look, Mr. Irwin. You're going to be here four days. You'd be better off to draw just $500 and see how it goes."

In the Midas Method, you need only a small percentage of wins against quite a few losses.

That wouldn't suit my system at all. If I were to lose the $500 at the table, by the time I asked for another $500 and the money was brought over, there could be a lapse of twenty minutes. That waiting period can be crucial; I may have been going through a series of losses at that particular point, and now I need additional money to carry me through the sequence. Had I kept playing, the sequence would have been back in my favour — in the Midas Method, you need only a small percentage of wins against quite a few losses.

There's more about junkets versus the consistent winner. Eventually, they don't want you. The junketeer receives from the casino a percentage of your losses at the tables. The majority of junketeers will not tell you they get a percentage, but I have been told otherwise. How else do they earn their salaries and the salaries of their staffs? Free airfare and hotel accommodation are enticing, but amount to very little in the grand scheme.

Some casinos give junket players non-negotiable chips — a coloured chip unlike the chips that the other players in the casino are using. These peg you as a junket player — whatever you win, you cannot cash in. Only if you have additional money in your pocket can you go to the casino next door. You're locked in. And remember, the casinos have only one thing going: eyes. They have people watching people, watching people watching people. There are dealers, there are inspectors, there are pit-bosses, there are head pit-bosses, there are head floor inspectors, there are casino managers, there are the floating people who walk around throughout the casino. And there is the "Eye in the Sky" — look up and you will see little plexiglass globes. You can't straighten your tie or put on your lipstick without someone looking down at you. (Casinos are really not too concerned about your cheating them. They worry that the dealers and the pit-bosses and the inspectors may be cheating the casino.)

We want losers on our trips; we do not want winners!

Meanwhile, there are also people who are walking around keeping tabs on who is at the pool and who's playing tennis. If you don't spend three or four hours at the tables daily, you just may be handed the hotel and the airfare bill — or be told not to come down on another junket. Is all this bother worth the price of a hotel ticket, a plane trip and meals? That's up to you to decide. But it's good to know the facts before signing up for your first junket.

A final thought. Years ago, when I contacted some junketeers about my gambling school, suggesting that their customers come down for some lessons, I received an interesting kind of reply. "Why," they asked, "should we send our players to your school to teach them how to play intelligently? We want losers on our trips; we do not want winners!" Over the years I have spoken with many people who have gone on junkets. Some were very upset and others had a great time.

I think it is only fair to you, that I recall one experience I had on a trip to the Caribbean. About a year ago a friend and I decided to go away for a week to Puerto Rico and the Bahamas on a gambling trip. At that time there was a junket going out of Toronto down to the Holiday Inn in Aruba, for a period of four days. The up-front money was $1,500 U.S. and they would pay the airfare, hotel accommodation, meals and drinks. We contacted them to find out if we could join the junket in Aruba. They said this was quite possible. So we took off on our own and went to the Bahamas and then to Puerto Rico and into Curacao playing in the casinos each night and finally arrived in Aruba the day prior to the junket coming in from Toronto. So we checked into the Holiday Inn, paid for our rooms, and proceeded to go into the casino. I was playing at the blackjack table betting maybe $100 to $200 on two or three different hands when the pit-boss came over to me and asked me what my name was and where I was from. I told them I was planning to join up with the junket that was coming in from Toronto the following day.

As it happened, this particular evening after playing at the table for about two hours I all of a sudden hit an extremely good run of cards and within approximately forty minutes, I had won $11,000. It created quite a flurry in the casino: here I was now playing three, four, five or six hands and I was winning almost all the time.

I was betting considerable amounts of money and winning considerable amounts of money so the pit-bosses were very close to my table. When I had decided that the trend of cards that I was drawing was slowly starting to change I decided that I had had enough for the evening. Now because I was going to be staying in that hotel for the next four days and playing in that particular casino as part of the junket which was starting the following day, I went to them with my chips and told them to just give me a marker and I would come in at 1:00 o'clock the next day and get my cash. They issued me a marker for the $11,000 and my friend and I left the casino and went upstairs to bed.

The next morning we had breakfast, went out and lay by the pool for a little while and finally at 1:00 o'clock I walked into the casino and pushed my $11,000 receipt to the cashier. After waiting for ten or fifteen minutes one of the casino people came over to me and said, "Well, you're on this junket that starts today are you not Mr. Irwin?" I said, "Yes, that's correct" and they said, "Well now it's customary for you to put up $1,500 U.S. front money for yourself and your partner has to put up $1,500 as well." I said I understood the arrangement and that when the junket arrives at 4:00 o'clock, we would place our money up along with everyone else. Well, they went away and for another ten or fifteen minutes I waited at the cashier's cage. Finally the same gentleman came back to me and he said, "Well, Mr. Irwin, we don't have any line of credit established for you here in the casino and we would really like you to have at least a $3,000 or $4,000 line of credit here so that you can play."

What it boiled down to was they were asking me to place, out of my $11,000, a $4,000 line of credit for myself, a $4,000 line of credit for my partner and $1,500 each, so in fact they were going to hold my $11,000 and let me draw against that money once the junket arrived in Aruba. Now you must understand that when I won the money the evening before it had absolutely nothing to do with any junket. I had only arrived in that casino a day earlier, and had stayed at that particular hotel only because I was going to be staying there anyway.

They would not give me my money until my junket arrived from Toronto which was expected at about 4:00 o'clock in the afternoon. You can imagine the attitude of my friend when

I went back upstairs to the room to relate to him that they wouldn't give me my money. Now we were not dependent on that money. We had a lot of other money put away in the safety deposit box, but it was the principle of the thing. After discussing it in the room we decided that the best thing to do was to wait until 4:00 o'clock until the junket arrived and speak to the junketeer. When 4:00 o'clock arrived, I went downstairs to the casino and called the junketeer off to the side and explained what had happened the evening before. He told me that he would speak with the casino people and for me to go back upstairs to my room and he would come up there. About a half hour later the man walked in and sat down on the edge of the bed. He had spoken to the casino management and they felt that I had not established a line of credit with them. He said that most people come down with more money than just $1,500 and that the casino would like to see me put up an additional amount of money as a line of credit in case I lost the $1,500, and that because I was a high-roller type player he would be prepared to take me downtown to a more exclusive place for dinner and wine and dine me and that he would see to it that I had a much better room in the hotel if I was prepared to leave my money there as a line of credit.

By this time both my friend and I were extremely upset with the attitude of both the junketeer and the casino management. I knew that the junketeer was thinking well, there's $11,000 there, and if that money is lost, whatever his percentage may be, maybe two, three, or four or five percent, it's going to be money not going into his pockets, so naturally he's going to fight as hard as he can to convince me to leave that

money in the casino. I explained to the junketeer that our only obligation was to put up
$1,500 each front money which we were pre-
pared to do and I wanted the other $8,000 im-
mediately.

He said he would go downstairs and speak
with them again and come back upstairs and
let us know. After waiting in the room for approximately two hours and he still had not
returned, I had decided that I would go downstairs and see if I could find him. I spent the
next half hour checking out all the various areas
in the hotel. I could not find him so I called his
room and was told that there was nothing he
could do about it at the moment since the assistant manager would not be in until 6:00
o'clock. I made arrangements with him to meet
me downstairs in the casino sharply at 6:15. At
6:15 I was in the casino and I had to wait another fifteen minutes for him to appear. Finally,
we rounded up the assistant manager and explained the situation to him. He told me there
was nothing he could do at that time and that
the casino manager would not be in until 11:00
o'clock in the evening.

Now in the interim period we had paid for
the hotel room for another day and decided that
we were not going to join up with the junket. If
we were going to do any gambling we would do
it at the other casinos in Aruba, and we would
get back the $11,000. I also went to the trouble
of finding out who was the head man of the
Gaming Commission in Aruba and I spoke to
the gentleman in the afternoon when I was first
informed that they would not give me my money.
I explained the circumstances to him and it was
left that if I did not get my money from the casino when I wanted it, I was simply to call him

again and he would guarantee that I would have payment within fifteen minutes.

My friend and I decided that we would give them until 11:00 o'clock and we would go to another hotel, have dinner and play in another casino.

At 11:00 we took a taxi back to the Holiday Inn and walked into the casino. The minute I walked into the casino area the junketeer came over to me and said how upset he was that I was not going to go along with what they were proposing, that I had created a bad image of him to the casino people and that he wanted me to leave my $11,000 there. I explained to him once again what our feelings were and that we had decided not to join the junket and to pay all our own expenses. We then went to the casino office and met with the casino manager and I told him that I had been speaking to the head of the Gaming Commission for the island. The minute I mentioned the man's name he authorized the payment of $11,000 in cash immediately to me.

I took the money and we stayed at the hotel for another evening since we had already paid for the room and decided that the next day we would then fly back to Puerto Rico.

CHAPTER 24

Birth of Las Vegas of the North

Between 1970 and 1980, gambling had gained a measure of respectability in Toronto. We now had lotteries being run by the government and off-track betting shops. More and more charity groups were using gambling equipment to run their Las Vegas and Millionaire Nights. The notion of gambling did not carry the stigma that it carried a decade before. In late 1979, the Canadian National Exhibition, which not so many years ago was closed on Sundays, considered the prospect of legalized gambling. It would certainly increase revenue and help to offset some of the losses suffered over the last few years. After having had many discussions with the principals at the CNE, I felt that if they were going to be issued a gaming licence for 1980, my organization certainly had the expertise to run the operation for them. As we do for a charity affair, we would leave all money-related matters in the hands of the Exhibition.

A number of charities were losing small fortunes.

My next concern at this time was to open another school. The time was right, I felt. Some of the charities that were operating casino nights were being taken to the cleaners by fly-by-night promoters making under-the-table deals and taking a percentage off the tables. The charity did not know how to run a successful casino night and they were dependent on the promoters. I observed what was happening at various functions and it was appalling. Nearly all the dealers knew little or nothing about the game of blackjack, and the players at the table were more astute than the dealers. In many cases, players were telling the dealer how the game should be played. Worse, the dealers had some of their own friends playing at the tables, and though the friends were losing on the cards they were drawing, the dealer was still paying them. As a result, a number of charities were losing small fortunes. My wife and I decided that now was the time to add some professionalism to the games. With the understanding that the CNE might be granted a licence to run casinos during the three weeks it was open, we felt that the timing was right. Not only could we train the proper staff for charitable functions, but we would have a proper facility for teaching the public how to play intelligently before they went to the casinos, at the Exhibition or anywhere else. We would also have a spot for training staff to man the casinos at the CNE.

I happened to be in the Bahamas for three or four days and ran into a friend who mentioned that there was a new plaza opening in suburban Toronto, with a Las Vegas-style nightclub bringing in top-rate shows. This would be a natural location for my school. On my return to Toronto I met some of the principals of the plaza, and was given some details about the 6th Dimension Club.

It was to be a high-class nightclub and, after

giving me a tour of the place, they showed me the empty space for lease upstairs. There were 12,000 square feet, 6,000 feet of which had been sectioned off for offices. It was January 5 and the club would be opening on a leap-year day, February 29.

My next step was to contact my partner, and together we looked at the site. My partner agreed that this would be a suitable location; we could tie in our venture with the nightclub. Basically, as we would be in business to train dealers as well as the general public, we did not require a liquor licence, but the availability of drinks at the nearby club was certainly a bonus. We could put together packages for dinner, a show and an evening upstairs in the casino, where the public could gamble with non-negotiable chips and be taught the elements of blackjack, roulette, baccarat and dice. We signed the lease — 6,000 square feet, 10 years — and my partner and I agreed that my wife and I would design and put together our premises.

I had been travelling the casino world for twenty years, and I knew what the public wanted.

We had every reason to be optimistic. The time was right — Toronto had come of age. The management was right — I had been travelling the casino world for twenty years, and I knew what the public wanted. And the location was right — we shared a plaza with a stunning half-million-dollar nightclub and we were a short drive from some of Toronto's most affluent — and youthful — neighbourhoods. With our optimism, we decided to make our casino school into a showpiece. I was to spend the rest of January, February, and March working toward our official opening date: April 21, 1980.

The first puncture in our balloon happened with the February 29 opening of the nightclub. The waitresses were beautiful and the room was stunning, but loveliness itself does not serve drinks and dinner with panache. Opening night was chaotic. To say nothing of the difficulties going on within the management of the club. The day after the debut, the club was being carried by one individual alone — meaning even less expertise. As we geared up for our own opening, the situation downstairs was deteriorating quickly.

Meanwhile, the landlord was having some problems with the mortgage company. And with the tradespeople. He was issuing bad cheques, not explanations. And here we were opening a posh gaming school while tradespeople were running about with their NSF cheques. The last thing we needed was the stigma of being associated with the nightclub downstairs.

The situation grew worse from day to day, reaching the point where we stopped sending our groups to the nightclub. And what would happen at our own opening? It was conceivable that by then the club could close. Dare we plan on hooking up with the club for our gala opening? For peace of mind, I made an arrangement with the landlord to rent the nightclub for one day. I would put in my own staff as chefs, bartenders, waiters and waitresses; would stock the place with beverages and operate the nightclub for the day of our opening.

By now, we had sent out invitations — not only to the Prime Minister but to the Attorney General's Office, the Provincial Police, the

RCMP, the Metro Toronto Police Department, and other notable politicians and dignitaries. It was important, for obvious reasons, that they learn that what we were doing was totally honest.

Two days before our grand opening, someone, apparently not very happy with the nightclub, forced some towels down one of the vacuum toilet systems. Unhappily, this meant that all the toilet facilities throughout the plaza would not be operative. Meanwhile, none of the tradespeople would come in to service the toilet system because they had not been paid by the landlord. At 5:00 PM on the day of our opening — 300 very important customers would be arriving in an hour — we made a special arrangement with the tradespeople. We would pay them directly if only they would get the toilets going again. They did.

Our opening night was an immense success.

For the next two weeks, while our business boomed, the club downstairs was having increasing woes. The writing was on the wall. It was inevitable that new people would come in and turn the place into a strip joint. After rounds of discussions, we decided to put in an offer ourselves for taking over the nightclub downstairs.

We put in an offer for $650,000 to buy out the premises. Two days later, the landlord came back with a counter offer of $900,000, extremely high considering the risk involved — it was impossible to figure out how much debt there was against the place, for no records or books had been kept. For the next week or two we continued the negotiations. On May 14 I was informed by the landlord's solicitor that the club was going to be closed the following day. Did I wish to make one further proposal? My partner and I decided that we would be interested in a management-type contract, and so offered to take over and manage the premises by investing our own money in the club for a period from May 15 through December 31. At the end of the year, we would negotiate with all the creditors. Having a clear picture then of the financial position of the club, we would be able to make a reasonable offer to buy it out. The landlord and his solicitor were agreeable to the arrangement, and at 1 AM on May 15, we took over the club.

At this time, about 100 people were active in my operation upstairs, and among the staff were experienced bartenders, chefs, waiters and waitresses. It was quite easy to take over at 1 AM on May 15, do a complete inventory, and open the next day for business. We decided to remain with the Las Vegas shows. For the next two and a half months, my days were spent negotiating with the creditors who were coming out of the woodwork. Evenings until 2:00 AM were spent in the nightclub.

On August 26, we had accumulated all the information related to the debt against the nightclub. We had an audit prepared and learned that the operation was $762,000 in the red. Calculations told us that if we were going to purchase the nightclub, we would have to take in a further $26,000 weekly for the next six years in order to retire the creditors. We decided to take the traditional course — to let the place go into receivership and then look forward to buying it back when it was clean of all debts. On the morning of August 26, we returned the keys to the landlord, removing the equipment we had placed in the operation. At 9:30 AM the doors were padlocked by the receiver and the club was placed in receivership on behalf of the creditors.

That was the situation till we could take over the club. I was sitting upstairs with an operation costing $4,000 a month in rent. A store-front operation for our rental department was costing another $1,200. Meanwhile, with no facilities for dinner and drinks, it was becoming increasingly difficult to keep the public coming in for lessons. Add to this one major blow: the plaza was being placed under power of sale because the landlord could not meet his commitments to the mortgage company. Finally, after two months of taking in $2,000 monthly and paying $5,000, my partner and I looked at the choices: walk out and leave almost a quarter of a million dollars of leasehold improvements behind us, or sit for the next year or two while the mess downstairs was cleared up through the courts. We decided to opt for the first choice. Which was not to say that we were giving up the ghost.

Rather than have the public come to us, we would take our entertainment to them. I had my solicitors check the various aspects of the criminal code to determine if it was legal to put blackjack tables into licenced premises — the customers could play at a table with no obligation to buy a drink. They could not play for money. If they did not know how to play blackjack, we would have our staff teach them. When they visited a real casino, they would minimize their losses because they now had some experience in playing.

We turned our backs on a dream.

My lawyers informed me that putting blackjack tables into lounges was perfectly legal, provided there was no money changing hands from one person to another. So with that in mind, I decided that rather than lose money in a plaza location, I would walk away from the white elephant. One of the saddest days of my life was October 27, when I walked into my wife's office and told her that I had decided to close down our dream. We had spent countless hours investing our energy and knowledge to put together a first class operation. But Jaye knew in her heart that we really had no other choice. On October 28, 1980, I called in additional staff and we prepared to close down our operation at 72 Steeles Ave. West. We turned our backs on a quarter of a million dollars of improvements. We turned our backs on a dream. Now it was time to start over again.

CHAPTER 25

Introducing a new form of entertainment

The Waldorf Astoria Hotel in downtown Toronto was experiencing a problem faced by other respectable hotels in the country: how to get people into its lounges. The economy had slowed down, and public taste was changing. Strippers and mud wrestlers and wet T-shirt contests were bringing in people, but many lounges were reluctant to put in that form of entertainment, and were looking for something more sophisticated in order to keep the public happy and drinking.

I met with a partner of the Waldorf Astoria, discussed my operation, brought him up to date with my lawyer's news that my blackjack tables and I could go into licenced premises quite legally. His own lawyer agreed that there would be no violations, and we began to set up an elaborate gaming room in the Pompeii Court of the Waldorf Astoria.

Our staff worked like beavers, and in early November we opened at the Pompeii Court. The first week was a trial period during which people could come in and view the operation. The attitude of the public was highly positive, and the tables were busy every evening from 5:00 till 11:00, as we taught baccarat, roulette and blackjack. Soon we were happily settled into the Waldorf Astoria, with a training facility operating on the fifth floor for the training of dealers.

The partner of the Waldorf, who was also a friend, invited me to join him on a short holiday in Las Vegas. He knew what I had been going through these last weeks, and suggested I take the time to relax and clear my head a bit. My wife agreed, and I knew that in her hands and in the hands of my staff, the operation would run smoothly.

As the flight took off from Toronto to Las Vegas I had the opportunity to reflect on how long it had been since I had been in a casino — an astonishing six months. I stretched my legs, relaxed, and looked forward to having a break from the pressures of the past six months. It was not to last very long.

The problem had nothing to do with the results at the tables. Quite the contrary. But it seemed that I had no sooner laid my head down on the pillow that first night when the telephone rang — at three in the morning. It was my buddy, who had found a message in his hotel room for me to phone my wife urgently.

Jaye was waiting for my call, and she was terribly upset. At five that evening, the manager of the Waldorf Astoria had walked into her office and said that the casino games downstairs in the Pompeii Court would have to be taken out immediately. He did not offer a reason — she should speak to the hotel partner who had remained in Toronto. When Jaye tried to reach him, he had gone for the day, so she stayed in the Pompeii Court till 11:00 PM explaining to people that there had been an electrical problem with some of the lighting we were putting in, but the games should be operating in a day or two. I told Jaye that I would be back to her after I had spoken to the partner in Las Vegas.

My buddy was not only a partner of the hotel but also had the liquor licence. He had spoken to his lawyers prior to our putting in the games and had been assured that everything was completely legal. Therefore, I could not grasp why all of a sudden the tables had to be taken out. When I found my friend in the casino and informed him about the call from Jaye, he suggested that I immediately call his partner in Toronto, regardless of the hour. What I learned from his partner was that his lawyer had called him late in the afternoon, suggesting that the tables be taken out. The weekend was coming up — we could not sort anything out then — so he suggested that I enjoy my holiday and, when I came back, get together with him and his lawyer. We would sit down and iron out whatever the problem was.

I immediately got hold of my buddy and he suggested that we should meet right away. At four in the morning, in the deli of the MGM Grand, I learned that one of the partners had a case before the courts coming up in February.

I understood the problem immediately. The lawyer wanted the tables out of there because the last thing in the world that they needed was a set-up that might create a problem with the police department. I contacted my lawyer and my wife to bring them up to date and arrange for a meeting when I returned.

The remainder of the day I spent lazing around the pool, and walking through the hotels, thinking about my next move and about the $12,000 I had just spent on the Pompeii

Court. When I awoke the next morning I knew what my next step would be. I was now able to enjoy the casinos, and by the time I was on the plane Monday afternoon, I had won back the investment made on the Waldorf Astoria at the casinos.

At our meeting the next day I was told again about the upcoming trial. The last thing the accused needed, his lawyer told me, was gambling tables in his establishment — he had to be lily white prior to the trial. I was in total agreement, but had I been informed prior to my investment I could have saved $12,000. I agreed to remove the tables, and the lawyer let me know that he believed my concept to supply tables to the lounges seemed a perfectly legal form of entertainment. If I wished, he would be prepared to work on my behalf to see that I was able to carry on with my plan of furnishing tables in other licenced premises.

CHAPTER 26

Pilot project in licenced premises

In July 1980, I tried to meet the police department and the Liquor Control Board to discuss the nature of our operations. The police department refused to sit down with us. The Liquor Control Board granted me an interview on August 23 and I informed its panel, chaired by Mr. Rice, of my intentions. They had remained aloof, with Mr. Rice remarking that he didn't believe anybody in the lounges would be interested in learning how to play blackjack. He had been to Las Vegas himself but never gambled at the tables — and he felt that he was typical of the general public. After spending several hours explaining that Toronto would benefit from a gambling school — perhaps $30 million leaves the city annually for the casinos of Vegas and the Caribbean — I politely told the panel that my present purpose was not to ask their permission — we had both agreed that the Liquor Board had no jurisdiction over what form of entertainment goes into licenced premises — but to inform them of my plans and of my legal position. I was prepared to work with them one hundred percent, so that they could monitor all that we were doing. Three days after my meeting, I received a letter from Mr. Rice's office requesting that I write out in detail what we had discussed. I did so immediately, and the report was sent by courier. I have never received a reply back from the Liquor Control Board or from Mr. Rice's office to this day.

Perhaps $30 million leaves the city annually for the casinos of Vegas and the Caribbean.

It was now the Christmas season of 1980, and my lawyers were presently reviewing all aspects of the law while we continued to train staff and provide entertainment for the various corporations we had been serving for the last fourteen years. We were going into hotels where people could drink at the tables and play with funny money — all perfectly legal.

My solicitors and I came to the conclusion that although putting our tables into the lounges was legal, I should nevertheless inform the lounge operators that there was a possibility the police could walk in and charge them with running a gaming house. Simply, there was nothing in the criminal code that said we could or could not put the tables in; hence, the police might try to make this a test case before the courts, to allow them to decide whether or not a gaming operation could go into a licenced lounge.

At this point, two of my staff had gone out on their own, setting up a gaming operation in a licenced lounge. My lawyers suggested that we should wait for a few weeks, to see if the police were going to take any form of action against the competition. Three weeks went by, there had been no movement by the police department, and so I began to visit potential customers. Three days later seven lounges were ready and willing to put in the blackjack tables, among them the Crown and Mitre Tavern. Our hours there were from five to nine, but the next morning I received a call from the manager. There had been a lot of people upset when he closed the table at nine — could we have a second shift, from nine till one in the morning? That was no problem, and a day later the manager was requesting another table. In the first week of operation, liquor sales revenue at the tavern had increased from $1,100 to $3,700. Customers were obviously enjoying the opportunity of coming up to the tables and sitting down, either with or without a drink — there was no obligation — and drawing twenty chips from the dealer. If they wanted instruction, fine; if not, they would proceed to play blackjack. If they lost the twenty chips they would draw an additional twenty, and at no time did it cost anything to draw chips or play at the table. Once a player realized that he was not winning, he would usually ask the dealer for individual instruction. The average individual entering a casino to play blackjack has about a 16 percent to 20 percent chance of winning. With the kind of basic education we offered — when to draw, how to draw, how to split cards, when to double-down, when to take insurance — he would now have a 49½ percent chance of success. (The house still has the half percent edge.)

We were providing education along with entertainment, with the result that customers chose to stay around a little longer and spend a little more on their bar bill.

We had been operating for about two weeks

when, one evening while I was sitting at home relaxing by the television, my beeper went off. The Crown and Mitre Tavern had now been raided by the police department. After the shock wore off, I then moved into action, phoning the newspapers, radio stations, the television news departments. For half a year the police had refused to sit down and discuss what we were proposing; now, they were charging the Crown and Mitre with running a gaming house. The statement from the police to the press was that they had collected three-hundred-plus-dollars — but they did not explain that this was cash from the cash register, representing receipts from drinks sold to the general public. The police also stated that because we were giving away a prize, that meant a gaming house was in operation. In fact, it was clearly stated on a blackboard that we were only taking the names of people, who, we felt, had won the most chips that evening; when we were advised that we could legally give a prize, they would be contacted. One of the undercover policemen who had come into the tavern during our two-week period had won the most chips one evening — and no prize had been awarded to him.

The minute I heard of the Crown and Mitre raid, I had my staff go around to our other six locations and pull out all the blackjack tables. Now that we had one case before the courts, that would be sufficient. I went to the police station myself, in case I had to bail out any of my staff. Once there, I was ushered into a room and charged with operating a gaming house. Also formally charged were my dealers, six found-ins, the manager of the Crown and Mitre, his bartender and his waitress. We were all released on our own recognizance, to appear for finger-printing and the trial.

On June 7, 1981, all of us pleaded Not Guilty. The case was remanded for trial.

Christmas came early in 1981. On December 7 we were all acquitted of all the charges against us. The ruling legally gave me the opportunity of putting my blackjack tables out into licenced premises.

I still believed that it was important to sit down with the police department and explain to them exactly how I proposed to go about our business. They felt that with the holiday season upon us, it was best to have our meeting after the first of the year. During this interim period the police department had an opportunity to appeal the provincial court's decision, and in calling them on January 5, 1982, to set a meeting they explained that they were appealing the decision. The department felt that the judge had erred in his interpretation of the law.

As far as our lawyers were concerned, we could go out and operate in the lounges because we had legally won the decision until the ruling was either overturned or upheld. Rather than go to a tavern owner and explain that we had gone to court and had won our case, but that they still may be bothered by the police, we decided not to upset the apple cart. We should await the appeal court decision.

In late March I was advised that the appeal court would be hearing our case on May 19, 1982, and on that day my wife and I went to court. On that afternoon we were told to come back the next day, and on May 20 our case was heard before the appeal courts. The presiding judges, Judges Goodman, Corey, and Martin decided to reserve judgment.

Finally, on Friday September 17, 1982, the

IN THE SUPREME COURT OF ONTARIO
COURT OF APPEAL
MARTIN, GOODMAN AND COREY JJ.A.

between:
HER MAJESTY THE QUEEN
Appellant

and

**ARTHUR BRUCE IRWIN,
DAVID ROBERT GARVIN,
ROBERT JOHN OLIVER, and
TERRELL MORGAN CRESS**
Respondents

John C. Pearson,
for the Crown, appellant.

L.A. Silverberg,
for the respondents,
Arthur Irwin and Robert Oliver.

R.H. Shekter,
for the respondent, Terrell Cress.

No one appearing for the
respondent, David Garvin.

Heard: May 20 and 21, 1982.

GOODMAN J.A.:

This is an appeal by the Crown from the acquittal of
the four respondents on December 7, 1981 by Provincial Judge T. Mercer on a joint charge that they:

> . . . during a four day period commencing June 1st
> and ending June 4th in the year 1981 at the Munici-
> pality of Metropolitan Toronto in the Judicial Dis-
> trict of York, did keep a common gaming house at
> 765 Mount Pleasant Road, Toronto, contrary to the
> *Criminal Code.*

I am, accordingly, of the view that the tavern proprietor or managers (as well as the players) cannot
be said to have been engaged in gambling or gaming
within the meaning of those words as used in the
various authorities referred to above. They are in
precisely the same position as the licenced proprietor
in the *McCollom* case. It is, accordingly, my opinion
that the Crown failed to prove that ''gaming'' or
''wagering'' took place in the tavern premises. In so finding I have kept in mind the provisions of s. 180(1)(c)
of the *Code* which would normally be applicable to a
case such as this. It is my view, however, that the facts
agreed upon by the parties render this subsection
inapplicable in the present instance.

In the result, for the above reasons, the appeal
is dismissed.

decision was handed down by the presiding judges — a unanimous decision by all three judges dismissing the crown's appeal.

This decision by the appeal courts now has opened the door for a new form of entertainment to be placed in licenced premises across Canada. As I have the expertise of gaming instruction as well as trained personnel in all forms of casino gaming it is now my intention to introduce this new form of entertainment into very selective establishments.

I have been in the gaming business for the last 23 years. It has been a fascinating life.

It has not been my intention to entice one to gamble at any time. However, as years go by, times change, and today Casino gaming has become an accepted form of entertainment.

Having read this far, you're probably anxious to try out the Midas Method. If there is anything that is not clear, or if you feel you need any further explanation of the system, please write me a letter. My address is Casino Gaming Instruction Inc, Box 59, Thornhill, Ontario, Canada L3T 3N1. Since you took the time to read my book, I'll return the favour and answer your letter personally.

CHAPTER 27

The rules for riches — memory, not magic

The time elapsed between the death of my uncle and the publication of this book has been long enough to change my life and give me an education I'm most anxious to pass along to anyone who likes to play in casinos.

I'd be lying if I said I've never lost. But when I did lose, it wasn't the system that failed. It was either myself (by faulty calculation) or cheating and the art of the "mechanic."

It wouldn't be fair to the reader, or to the system, to publish it without explaining the pitfalls in the green felt jungle.

I once told a casino manager that I had a foolproof system. "Great," he laughed, "more power to you. But, you know, we don't worry. You may be able to stick to the rules of your system. The next guy probably won't. We'll be waiting for him to give us back the money you win."

But even a foolproof system is still the tool of a very frail animal.

He enlarged on his theme. He said that there have been countless systems tried. Most have inherent weaknesses. But even a foolproof system is still the tool of a very frail animal.

The mental strain of calculating in the din of a casino often makes a system break down. But more often, when the system player finds he's winning, he makes the mistake of gambling on his luck. He usually loses.

The casino manager even admitted that a lot of system players have been separated from their faith and their cash by mechanics. There's no protection I know against cheating. There are, however, some rules that can help:

a) Don't stay very long in any one club, and don't frequent the same club too often. Anonymity isn't easy with my system — but you can avoid the kind of notoriety that invites the house to use underhanded methods to get rid of you.

b) Be satisfied with winning a small amount of money at a sitting.

c) Spend no more than about twenty minutes at any one table. Be on your guard when the wheelman or dealer is changed just as you sit down — and doesn't change for forty minutes. The normal shift for a dealer at any specific table is approximately thirty minutes, depending how busy the club is. If a dealer stays for a much shorter or longer period than thirty minutes — *beware*. In all probability he has been assigned to you.

I won't say you'll break the bank, or even the table. But if you play as I suggest, and follow my system strictly, you can and will make money.

The casinos will always be there.

Read the system carefully. Buy yourself a small

roulette wheel and practise. For those who can't find a roulette wheel buy one, two or three decks of cards. Shuffle them up together, and as you turn a card bet whether it is red or black, odd or even.

It's fun even in the dry runs — and it will help prepare you for the big greenfelt battle-field ahead.

APPENDIX

How to play the games

Gambling rules for roulette.

You exchange any desired amount of money for chips (gambling discs) at the cash desk and proceed to any gambling table which is in operation. If no seat is available, you may also take part in the game when standing and apply to the supervisor for the next seat to become vacant.

As soon as the turning croupier (also called the paying or top hat croupier) calls out: "Please, make your stakes," you place your stake on one or more chances which you think may bring you a win. When the croupier is turning the ball, you may still make your stakes until he says: "No more bets." When the ball has jumped into a number section, the croupier will point to this number with the rateau (rake), call out this number and at the same time all winning chances. The losses are raked in and the gains paid out in a certain order, and the next game can start. Money for the continuation of the game may also be changed at the gambling tables.

Roulette.

Each player receives different color chips. He may play them on red or black; odd or even; combinations of numbers or a single number.

The different bets, and their payoffs, are outlined below.

AMERICAN ROULETTE

Roulette payoffs.

When you bet on	You place your chips	It pays
(A) Red or Black		even money
(B) Odd or Even	in Odd or Even Box	even money
(C) 18 Numbers	in 1-18 or 19-36 Box	even money
(D) 12 Numbers	at End of Any Long Column	2 to 1
(E) 12 Numbers	in First 12, Second 12 or Third 12 Box	2 to 1
(F) 6 Numbers	on Dividing Line at Side	5 to 1
(G) 5 Numbers	Line Dividing 0, 00 from 1, 2 and 3	6 to 1
(H) 4 Numbers	in Cross Between 4 Numbers	8 to 1
(I) 3 Numbers	on Line at Side of 3 Numbers	11 to 1
(J) 2 Numbers, or 0 and 00	on Line Between 2 Numbers	17 to 1
(K) Single Number on Number		35 to 1

Player declares the price he or she wants the chips to stand for.

1. 35-1 on all numbers, also 0 and 00.
2. 17-1 on Two numbers, such as 9 and 12.
3. 11-1 on Three numbers, such as 16, 17, 18.
4. 8-1 on Four numbers, such as 23, 24, 26, 27.

5. 5-1 on Six numbers, such as 28, 29, 30, 31, 32, 33.
6. 2-1 on all bets placed in First, Second or Third column.
7. 2-1 on all bets placed in First, Second or Third dozen.

AMERICAN VERSION OF ROULETTE WHEEL

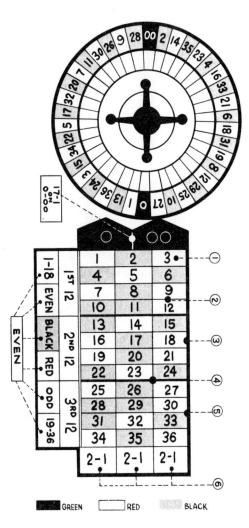

GREEN   RED   BLACK

EUROPEAN ROULETTE GAME AND WINNING PLAN

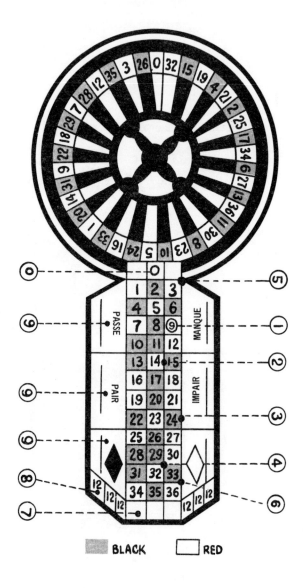

BLACK   RED

EUROPEAN ROULETTE (FRENCH)

Winning plan	It pays
1. A single number................	35 to 1
2. 2 connecting numbers...........	17 to 1
3. 3 numbers across...............	11 to 1
4. Square of 4 numbers.............	8 to 1
5. First 4 numbers (0, 1, 2, 3)........	8 to 1
6. 6 numbers across................	5 to 1
7. Column of 12 numbers............	2 to 1
8. First middle or last 12............	2 to 1

9. Simple chances:

Pair or Impair (i.e. even or odd no.)....	1
Red or Black......................	1
Manque, nos. 1-18.................	1
Passe, nos. 19-36..................	1

0. ZERO: All stakes on simple chances are by choice either en prison (blocked) or lose one-half. If ZERO appears twice in succession, all blocked stakes on simple chances will become double blocked. If ZERO appears three times in succession, all double-blocked stakes will go to the bank in full. If any stake is blocked at ZERO, the owner of that stake can only place again on the same chance that amount which in addition to one-half of the blocked stake respectively to one-quarter of the double-blocked stake will reach the maximum of the respective table.

				TABLE OF ADJACENT NUMBERS				
12	35	3	26	O	32	15	19	4
5	24	16	33	1	20	14	31	9
15	19	4	21	2	25	17	34	6
7	28	12	35	3	26	O	32	15
O	32	15	19	4	21	2	25	17
30	8	23	10	5	24	16	33	1
2	25	17	34	6	27	13	36	11
9	22	18	29	7	28	12	35	3
13	36	11	30	8	23	10	5	24
1	20	14	31	9	22	18	29	7
11	30	8	23	10	5	24	16	33
6	27	13	36	11	30	8	23	10
18	29	7	28	12	35	3	26	O
17	34	6	27	13	36	11	30	8
16	33	1	20	14	31	9	22	18
3	26	O	32	15	19	4	21	2
23	10	5	24	16	33	1	20	14
4	21	2	25	17	34	6	27	13
14	31	9	22	18	29	7	28	12
26	O	32	15	19	4	21	2	25
24	16	33	1	20	14	31	9	22
32	15	19	4	21	2	25	17	34
20	14	31	9	22	18	29	7	28
36	11	30	8	23	10	5	24	16
8	23	10	5	24	16	33	1	20
19	4	21	2	25	17	34	6	27
28	12	35	3	26	O	32	15	19
25	17	34	6	27	13	36	11	30
22	18	29	7	28	12	35	3	26
31	9	22	18	29	7	28	12	35
27	13	36	11	30	8	23	10	5
33	1	20	14	31	9	22	18	29
35	3	26	O	32	15	19	4	21
10	5	24	16	33	1	20	14	31
21	2	25	17	34	6	27	13	36
29	7	28	12	35	3	26	O	32
34	6	27	13	36	11	30	8	23

■ GREEN   ▭ RED   ▨ BLACK

Baccarat — Chemin de Fer.

One of royalty's favorite pastimes, chemin de fer, and its casino counterpart, baccarat, are joined to bring you baccarat-chemin de fer.

The object of the game, which is played strictly according to the rules outlined here, is to bet on either of two sides: the bank or the player (against the bank), whichever you feel will have the highest point.

The point is reached by totaling the cards dealt to either the player or the bank, but using only the last digit if the total is a two-digit number. (For example, a 1 3 10 gives point 4; a 6 7 8 gives point 1.)

The croupier always represents the player side, and the bettors or participants take turns representing the bank side.

The player side (represented by the croupier) receives two cards dealt from the shoe by the participant whose turn it is to represent the bank, who also deals himself two cards.

The player side, acting first, turns his cards face up and having point 8 or 9, gets an immediate decision; having point 6 or 7 stands; and having point 5 or less, asks for another card.

The bank side then turns cards face up and gets an immediate decision with point 8 or 9, stands with point 7, and draws another card with 6 or less if the accompanying chart so indicates. Banker side, if player side stands, always draws on 5 or less and always stands on 6 or 7.

RULES

PLAYER		BANKER		
HAVING		HAVING	DRAWS WHEN GIVING	DOES NOT DRAW WHEN GIVING
		0-1-2	ALWAYS DRAWS	
1-2-3-4-5-10	DRAWS A CARD	3	1-2-3-4-5-6-7-9-10	8
6-7	STANDS	4	2-3-4-5-6-7	1-8-9-10
8-9	TURNS CARDS OVER	5	4-5-6-7	1-2-3-8-9-10
		6	6-7	1-2-3-4-5-8-9-10
		7	STANDS	
		8-9	TURNS CARDS OVER	

CRAP TABLE

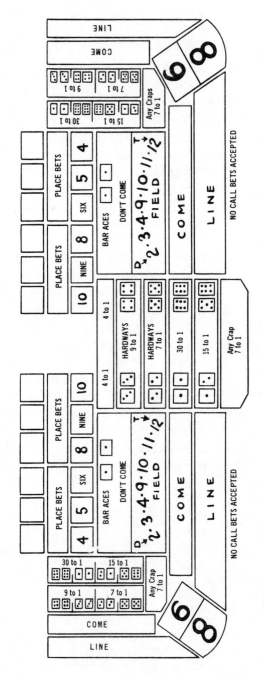

* D No. 2 on field pays DOUBLE
* T No. 12 on field pays TRIPLE

Craps.

Craps is a form of dice that is fast and simple —an exciting, pulse-quickening game that is easily understood and universally liked. Study the table diagram. There are different layouts for a crap table, but this type of layout is most familiar to the clientele.

PASS LINE.

An even-money bet; you're betting with the shooter (either yourself or any other). On the first roll you win if a natural—7 or 11—comes up; you lose on craps (2, 3 or 12). Any other total that may show on the dice (4, 5, 6, 8, 9, or 10) is the point. To win after a point is thrown, the point must be thrown before a 7 appears.

COME BETS.

This is a bet made after the Point has been established and is good for the next throw of the dice. If a 7 or 11 appear you win, if a 2, 3, or 12 appear you lose, any other number is placed in the proper box and if you wish you may take the odds. You can continue to play the Come or Don't Come on each new throw until the point has either been won or lost.

DON'T COME BETS.

The opposite of COME BETS played with the same procedure described above.

DON'T PASS.

The rules in this are the same as above, except that you are playing against the shooter (yourself or any other), and the game is reversed for you. You lose if a 7 or 11 comes up on the first roll; you win on 3 or 12. If a 2 (two aces) is thrown, it's a stand-off and you neither win nor lose. If a point is established and then made, you lose; if a 7 comes before the point is made, you win.

BOXES.

At any time the game is in progress you may decide to bet boxes, which are 4, 5, 6, 8, 9 and 10. You may bet either on the number or against the number in any of the boxes.

If you bet on the number in any box, that number must come up before 7 for you to win. The house gives you the odds.

If you bet against the number in any box, 7 must come up before that number is thrown for you to win. You give the house the odds.

Correct odds of 2 to 1 on 4 or 10; 3 to 2 on 5 or 9; 6 to 5 on 6 or 8 will be given or taken provided a five percent commission accompanies the bet.

Blackjack / 21.

You play against the dealer. The object is to draw cards totaling 21, or as close as possible, without going over, or bust. The dealer gives two cards face up to each player, one face up and one face down to himself, after all bets have been placed. Aces count 1 or 11, picture cards are 10, all other cards count their face value.

If you have Blackjack (an Ace with a picture card or 10), it beats any other combination except a dealer Blackjack, and you win 3 to 2 for your bet. If the dealer has Blackjack too, it's a stand-off — you neither win nor lose.

If neither of you has Blackjack, you decide from your cards whether to draw more cards (Hit) or to not draw cards (Stand). You may take as many cards as you wish until you think you have a score closer to 21 than the dealer will have. The dealer must draw on a total of 16 or under, and must stand on 17.

If your total is closer to 21 than the dealer's total — you win even money.

If your total is lower than the dealer's — you lose.

If you tie with the dealer — it's a stand-off.

If you go over 21 — you lose.

DOUBLING DOWN.

In Las Vegas you may double your original bet on any two cards dealt you.

In Europe, Atlantic City and the Caribbean you may double your original bet only if the first two cards dealt you total either 9, 10 or 11, and even in some casinos you can only double your bet on 10 and 11.

In doubling your original bet you receive only one card extra for in this situation you are looking for a 10 or an Ace.

Out of a 4 deck shoe you have 64 cards with a value of 10 . . . 16 of everything else. Out of a 6 deck shoe you have 96 cards with a value of 10 . . . 24 of everything else. Out of an 8 deck shoe you have 128 cards with a value of 10 . . . 32 of everything else.

SPLIT BETS.

You may split your first two cards into separate hands if they are a pair. Even if you have a Jack and a Queen, you can split them in some casinos as they both have a value of 10 although they are not natural pairs. You must play the hand to your right first after splitting and only then when you have finished playing the right hand do you play the left hand. You must place the same amount of money as originally bet on the second hand.

Some casinos will allow you to split again should you draw a third card to match the first two, however, it is not common throughout the gaming industry.

You must always split a pair of Aces and should you draw a card with a value of 10 to one or both you are only paid even money. You are paid 3 to 2 only on a Blackjack (Ace and 10) consisting of the first two cards dealt to you.

When splitting Aces you are allowed one card only to each Ace, however, in splitting any other pair you may draw as many cards as you wish.

INSURANCE.

If the dealer has an Ace showing you may take insurance by placing half your original bet in the insurance box. If the dealer has a 10 in the hole you are paid 2 to 1 for your insurance bet. If he has no Blackjack you lose your insurance bet.

Insurance is a sucker bet and the dealer will only have it 15 times out of 49 hands with the Ace up. It is only a fair bet if you have a Blackjack and should only be taken at that time.

The secret of success

Playing the games and playing the method.

Any system is really a control on your method of betting. It is absolutely impossible for you to win every time. However, it *is* possible to control your money and control the amount you are betting. This proves extremely helpful if you are running into a considerable number of losses.

This book has not been written to entice you to gamble, but to increase your chances at the tables.

We will first preview the games, then apply the Method.

Roulette.

The Three Column Method.
This is a method that I picked up during my travels through Europe. I have played it myself from time to time and found that it will work successfully. It does, however, require a large bankroll if any great amount of money is to be made. And remember this: you can lose. I have found, however, that if played in moderation, your chances of leaving the tables a winner are in your favor.

To start, let us imagine that the ball has landed on the color red. Now looking at either the American or European version of the roulette wheel, you will notice that the column starting at (1) and running down to number 34 contains 6 reds as well as 6 blacks. Moving on to the middle column, starting at number 2 and running down to number 35, we now have 4 reds and 8 blacks. The third column, from 3 to number 36, has 8 reds and only 4 blacks.

You will also note that although the numbers are in the correct order, 1 2 3 4 5 6 7 to 36, the colors only seem to run in a red, black, red, black, red, black sequence. Number 11, which should be red if following a true pattern, is black. Number 19, further down, is red, not black; 29 is black, not the expected red.

Now that we have an idea of the columns, let us go a step further.

By watching the wheel spun for a free turn, we establish that the ball has landed in red. Count the number of reds in the first column (1 to 34). There are 6. In the second column there are only 4. In the third column there are 8. If we are to cover as many reds as possible — by playing two columns at the same time — we would pick the first and third, which gives us a total of 14 reds. (If we were to play the first and second, we would only be covering 10 reds.) You can see the advantage of playing the first and third columns — we have gained 4 reds over the first and second, and 2 reds over the second and third.

We have now established a type of pattern. If the ball has landed in red on our free spin, we would then place our bets in the first and third columns, giving us the greater number of reds covered for the next spin.

Should the ball have landed in the black, we would play the first and second columns, incorporating the greatest number of blacks.

Remember, we are not only covering the majority of reds or blacks. We are also covering the 14 blacks that appear in columns one and three, and the 14 reds in columns one and two.

We are now covering a total of 24 numbers, giving us 14 reds with 4 reds against us; and 10 blacks, with 8 blacks against us. Counting the single 0 and double 00 out of the 38 numbers on the layout, we are covering 24 numbers. This leaves 14 numbers against us.

No matter what two columns you play, you can only cover 24 numbers. But the key is not to cover the greatest amount of numbers, but the greatest number of colors.

The advantage to playing this method is that the payoff is 2 to 1.

Let us try a sample game and see what happens. Below is a record of 20 games played.

CHART ONE

RED	FREE SPIN
RED	
19 RED	
27 RED	
	6 BLACK
	11 BLACK
9 RED	
	4 BLACK
	24 BLACK
	10 BLACK
12 RED	
	6 BLACK
34 RED	
	20 BLACK
5 RED	
9 RED	
27 RED	
	10 BLACK
	2 BLACK
9 RED	
14 RED	
7 RED	

Having had our free spin with the color red winning, our bet would be $50 on the first and third columns. (This would give us 14 reds and 10 blacks.) Number 19 red wins, which is in the first column.

So we have won in the first column, and are paid off $100; we lost $50 in the third column. We are a $50 winner. Because 19 red won, we will now continue to play the first and third columns, covering again the greatest number of reds along with 10 blacks.

Number 27 red wins this time. Because 27 is in the third column, we have another win and another profit of $50. We now continue to play the first and third columns. At the end of the roll we see that 6 black hits. Six is in the third column, giving us another win: $100 in column three. However, we've lost $50 on column one, measuring a gain of $50.

Because black won, we will now switch from the first and third columns to the first and second columns, thereby covering the majority of blacks (along with 10 reds). We see that number 11 black wins. Because we have been playing the first and second columns, and because 11 is in the second column, we win another $100 and lose $50 — a profit of $50 again.

Now, because 11 black has hit, we stay with the first and second columns. Number 9 hits. We lose our money — $50 in the first column and $50 in the second — a total of $100.

Because red has hit, we now move our bets, placing $50 on the first column and $50 on the third column, once again covering the majority of reds. Number 4 wins, making us $100 from the first column and losing us $50 in the third. Still sticking with black by playing the first and second columns, we see that number 24 black hits; 24 is in the third column, so we lose $100.

Because the color is still black we stay with the first and second columns, giving us once again the advantage of the blacks. Number 10 in the black hits, giving us a win of $100 on the first column and a loss of $50 in the second.

Because it was black, we will now stay with the first and second columns. Number 12 red hits; 12 is in the third column not the ones we were playing — so we lose $100. Because 12 red has hit, we now move to the first and third columns, therefore giving us the advantage of reds. Number 6 in the black wins — $100 gained and $50 lost.

Because 6 black has hit, we now play the first and second columns, covering the most blacks. Number 34 red hits; 34 is in the first column, so our profit is $100 and our loss is $50. Because it was red, we will now play the first and third columns. Now, number 20 black hits — a loss of $100.

We now switch to the first and second columns. Number 5 red wins — we're up $50. Because it was red, we will go now to the first and third columns. Number 9 red wins — another $50 profit.

Because it was red, we stay with red, still covering the first and third columns, and number 27 red hits — another profit of $50. Because it was red, we stay with the first and third columns and we notice the next number up is 10 black, in the first column — another $50. Because it was black that won, we now play the first and second columns. Number 2 black hits — an additional $50 profit.

So we stay with the first and second columns, but 9 red hits — a loss on both the first and second columns of $50 apiece. Because red has hit, we now switch from the first and second to the first and third columns. Number 14 red hits. We are not covering the middle column where number 14 is located, so we lose another $100. Because it was 14 red, we stay with the first and third columns and find that number 7 red hits — a profit again of $50.

Out of the 20 spins on the wheel and by betting $50 each time, whether we won or we lost, on either one and three columns or one and two columns, we have gained a profit, after 20 rolls, of $100. Now we were $200 up at the end of the fourth roll, after beginning, so the idea of this system, pretty well, is that you set out to make a certain amount of dollars. Normally, if you make $200 or $300, you would quit. The amount of money you are betting determines how fast you will make this. Some people play the table limit. If the table limit is $500, they play until they are exactly $500 ahead. They could do this on the first spin of the wheel, or they could invest $5,000 — and still there is really no guarantee that they will make their $500 unless they are in a financial position to carry on with an unlimited amount of money until they have made their win of $500. Remember, always bet the same amount on each column you are playing.

18–10 Method.

The next system that I would like to discuss is the 18–10 method. Now, you will notice, by checking the roulette layout, that we have 18 reds and 18 blacks. We also have 18 odds and 18 evens, as well as 18 highs and 18 lows. If we were to place $50 on the black and any one of the black 18 numbers should come up, we would automatically win. If we were to place $50 on the odd and any one of the odd numbers should come up, we would win also. If we played both black and odd together, placing $50 on each one, and any black and odd number hit for that spin, we would win on both, therefore making $100. But let us say, for example, that number 19 should hit; 19 is red, so we would lose our $50 on the black but we would win on the odd — breaking even. Now by playing black and odd together, using the same amount of money on each one for a bet, we are covering 18 blacks plus 10 other odd numbers on the red. Because we are playing black, we are covering both the evens and the odds of black. That's why we don't have to worry about any of the black numbers. And by playing odd, we are covering all the odd numbers in red, which gives us another 10 numbers. Therefore, we are covering 28 numbers out of the 36, plus the 2 greens. Against us are 12 numbers. We have 28 numbers in our favour. Let us go back to the chart No. 1, where we ran off 20 games, and let's just see how we would do by playing the 18–10 method. Say that we start off by playing black and odd. We are playing this combination because it gives us 28 of the 36 numbers. If we were playing black and even we would only be covering 26 numbers against 28 playing black and odd. Therefore the advantage to us is to play black and odd or red and even.

Now let us put $50 on black and $50 on odd and see what happens. First, we have 19 red. We lose on black but win on odd, so we break even. By placing the same amount on black and odd our next number is 27 red. Once again, we break even. 6 black. Now we lose on odd and we win on black. Once again we break even. The next number is 11 black and now we win $100; we win on the black as well as on the odd. The next number is 9 red. Because we have odd completely covered we win on odd and lose on black — one has paid the other. The next number is 4 black — win on black, lose on odd.

Our next figure is 24 black — we break even. The next number is 10 black — we break even. The next number is 12 red — we lose $100. Our next figure is 6 black. By playing black and odd we win on one and lose on the other — we break even. Our next figure is 34 red — a $100 loss. At this point we are out of pocket $200. The next figure being 20 black, we win on one, lose on the other. The next figure is 5 red — breaking even again. The next number is 9 red — same thing. The next 27 red — break even. The next figure is 10 black — break even. The next is 2 black — we break even. The next is 14 red — lose $100.

The next figure is 7 red, so we don't make any money. And at the end of the 20 rolls, we have had 3 losses where we lost on both black and odd at the same time, and one win where we won on both at the same time. So adding our wins and our losses, we find at the end of these 20 spins, we are $200 in the hole.

Now, let us play red and even, placing $50 on each and using the same chart; same number of break-evens; 3 wins of $100 each; one loss of $100.

Now we will switch to playing a combination that covers 26 of the 36 numbers, therefore taking the disadvantage of an additional 2 numbers against us. Let us see how we would come out after the 20 games.

We are now playing black and even. Our first number up was number 19 red; therefore we lose $100. Our next number is 27 red; we lost another $100. 6 black wins $100. 11 black breaks even. 9 red loses $100. 4 black wins $100. 24 black wins $100. 10 black wins $100. 12 red breaks even. 6 black wins $100. 34 red breaks even. 20 black wins $100. 5 red loses $100. 9 red loses $100. 27 red loses $100. 10 black wins $100. 2 black wins $100. 9 red loses $100. 14 red breaks even. 7 red loses $100.

We have had 8 losses and 8 wins — breaking even at the end of 20 games.

Now let us play red and odd. Our first number is 19 red and we win $100. 27 red wins $100. 6 black loses $100. 11 black breaks even. 9 red wins $100. 4 black loses $100. 24 black loses $100. 10 black loses $100. 12 red breaks even. 6 black loses $100. 34 red breaks even. 20 black loses $100. 5 red wins $100. 9 red wins $100. 27 red wins $100. 10 black loses $100. 2 black loses $100. 9 red wins $100. 14 red breaks even. 7 red wins $100.

Again, we have had 8 wins and again we have had 8 losses so therefore, we have made nothing.

Now we are going one step further, supposing you wanted to play black and low against red and high. It would make no difference because you are only covering an additional 9 numbers, whether you are playing black and low, or black and high. Low meaning 1–18; High, 19–36. You are only covering the other 9 numbers if you should be playing red and low and red and high, so it isn't advantageous one way or the other. It's purely a guess.

Again, if you were to play even and high against even and low, you'll notice you're going to cover the same quantity of numbers, totaling 27, no matter which way you play it, therefore, it's really six of one and half a dozen of the other as to which one you would play. So the advantage that I have found in playing this method however, is, to play black and odd, rather than play black and even, gaining that extra 2 numbers and in turn, playing red and even against black and odd, rather than red and odd against black and even.

Wear out the dealer.

The next little system that we shall play is one which I call "Wear Out The Dealer." With this particular system we are now playing on the numbers straight up. That is, if you were to place a chip in the center of any one of the numbers, you would be paid off 35 to 1. If you were to place the chip between 2 numbers, say between 26 and 29, and either one of those 2 numbers should hit, you would get 17 to 1. Now you pick whatever 4 numbers you wish on the wheel, forgetting what is on the layout. By this I mean if you look at your roulette wheel, you will notice that number 33, 21, 6 and 18 are all side by side. Also 17, 32, 20 and 7 as well as 1, 13, 36 and 24. If you look at your layout and pick 4 numbers, like 1, 2, 3 and 4, your 1, 2, 3 and 4 on the roulette wheel are fairly well spaced out. This you don't want. Pick any 4 numbers which are grouped together side by side on the roulette wheel. Let us consider for this time that we will pick numbers 30, 11, 7 and 20.

30, 11, 7, 20

CHART No. 1

AMOUNT OF CHIPS BET ON EACH OF THE FOUR NUMBERS	REPEATED NO. OF TIMES	NO. OF CHIPS PLAYED
1 Chip	6 Times	24 Chips
2 Chips	5 Times	40 Chips
3 Chips	4 Times	48 Chips
4 Chips	3 Times	48 Chips
5 Chips	2 Times	40 Chips
TOTAL	20 Games	200 Chips

Now to play this game you can start with 3 different bankrolls. If you're carrying $200 you buy $200 worth of $1 chips. If you have $100 you buy 200—50¢ chips. If you have a $50 bankroll you buy 200 —25¢ chips. Now, to play, you will follow the chart 1 above. One chip, placed on each number, and you continue this procedure 6 times. Two chips on each number and you continue this 5 times. Three chips on each number you continue for 4 times. Four chips on each number and you continue 3 times. Five chips on each number and you continue 2 times. This will give you a total of 20 consecutive plays. During which time, if you should lose, 20 *times in a row,* you will have lost your $200 if you were playing with $1 chips. So keeping the chart above in mind we'll continue to play the game.

Now that we have picked the numbers 30, 11, 7 and 20, you will notice that by looking at the roulette wheel, these 4 numbers are grouped together. We will play with $1 chips and a $200 bankroll. You place one chip on each of the 4 numbers for the first spin of the wheel. If you lose, then you continue to bet one chip on these 4 numbers until you have done this 6 times. In the event of 6 consecutive losses, you would place 2 chips on each number and continue this procedure for 5 times—and so on, until we're putting 5 chips on each number, and you would repeat this twice. Now, if you did not win during this period, you would have lost your $200. However, let us suppose that we had 2 chips going on number 20 and, after a few spins of the wheel, we won. On our next bet, we would double the amount of chips on each number. If we won, we would double the amount of chips on each number once again. However, if we had experienced one win, with 2 chips on 20, and after having doubled the chips found that we lost, we would then revert back to the beginning by placing one chip on each number and continuing the same procedure 6 times. And so forth, until we had run through the complete sequence once again.

Now I am going to run off a few games, and let us see just what happens. Follow the charts below, and bet the method as suggested in chart 1 on page 195.

CHART 2

		BET	NUMBER	WON	LOST	TOTAL
	1	4.00	15B		4.00	– 4.00
	2	4.00	20B	35.00	3.00	28.00
Double		8.00	0		8.00	20.00
	1	4.00	5R		4.00	16.00
	2	4.00	32R		4.00	12.00
	3	4.00	5R		4.00	8.00
	4	4.00	31B		4.00	4.00
	5	4.00	21R		4.00	0.00
	6	4.00	5R		4.00	– 4.00
Two	1	8.00	34R		8.00	– 12.00
	2	8.00	16R		8.00	– 20.00
	3	8.00	20B	70.00	6.00	44.00
Double		16.00	26B		16.00	28.00
	1	4.00	22B		4.00	24.00
	2	4.00	25R		4.00	20.00
	3	4.00	6B		4.00	16.00
	4	4.00	1R		4.00	12.00
	5	4.00	32R		4.00	8.00
	6	4.00	34R		4.00	4.00
Two	1	8.00	20B	70.00	6.00	68.00
Double		16.00	15B		16.00	52.00
	1	4.00	35B		4.00	48.00
	2	4.00	19R		4.00	44.00
	3	4.00	18R		4.00	40.00
	4	4.00	15B		4.00	36.00
	5	4.00	36R		4.00	32.00
	6	4.00	15B		4.00	28.00
Two	1	8.00	28B		8.00	20.00
	2	8.00	14R		8.00	12.00
	3	8.00	17B		8.00	4.00
	4	8.00	00		8.00	– 4.00
	5	8.00	19R		8.00	– 12.00
Three	1	12.00	34R		12.00	– 24.00
	2	12.00	6B		12.00	– 36.00
	3	12.00	33B		12.00	– 48.00
	4	12.00	6B		12.00	– 60.00
Four	1	16.00	11B	140.00	12.00	68.00
Double		32.00	34R		32.00	36.00
		288.00		315.00	279.00	36.00

So we have now got one chip on each one of the 4 numbers—30, 11, 7 and 20—and number 15 black hits. Therefore, we lose. We now place one chip on each of the 4 numbers again. Number 20 black hits. Because we are playing one chip and are playing on number 20, we have been paid off 35 to 1. So we have won $35 on number 20 plus the dollar we bet, giving us $36. However, we have lost $1 on 30, $1 on 11, $1 on 7 plus $4 on previous roll—so we've lost $7. Our profit is $28. Now, because we won on 20 and we were betting one chip at that time, we now double up on each number with 2 chips, so we now have 2 chips riding on 7, 20, 11 and 30. Zero hit and we lost. Therefore, because we lost, after having doubled up, we now go back to the top of chart 1 using one chip on each number and run through this program 6 times. Our first time out, betting $4 on the spin, 5 red hits — we lose. Second time out, 32 red hits — we lose. Third time out, 5 red hits—we lose. Fourth time out, 31 black hits—we lose. Fifth time out, 21 red hits — we lose. Sixth time out and the final time out for one chip on each number, 5 red hits—and we lose. Because we've lost 6 times, at one chip on each, we now double to 2 chips on each number and come out to run through this procedure 5 times. Our first time out with 2 chips on each number, 34 red hits — for a loss. Second time out, 16 red hits—for a loss. Third time out, 20 black hits —we win. Being paid off 35 to 1 and having $2 on number 20, we have won a total of $70. Subtracting the $6 lost on the other 3 numbers, we have a net profit of $64 on this spin. At this point we are $44 ahead.

Because we have won on number 20, betting 2 chips on each, we now double to 4 chips on each and come out with number 26 black hitting for a loss. Because we lost after having doubled, we now return to the top of the chart, running through the first 6 times with one chip on each number. Number 22 black hits — we lose. Second time out, 25 red hits—we lose. Third time out, 6 black hits—we lose. Fourth time out, 1 red hits—we lose. Fifth time out, 32 red hits—we lose. Sixth time out, 34 red hits — we lose.

Because we have played it through 6 times and lost, we now change to 2 chips on each number and come out with an $8 bet on a spin of the wheel. Number 20 black hits, which is a win for us, paying us 35 to 1 and giving us a profit of $70. Subtract our losses of $46 and we make a net profit of $68.

Because we won, we now double up to 4 chips on each number, with $16 going on the spin, number 15 black wins—we lose. Because we lost, we now return to the top of the chart, betting one chip on each number, and number 35 black hits — we lose. Second time out, 19 red hits — we lose. Third time out, 18 red hits — we lose. Fourth time out, 15 black hits—we lose. Fifth time out, 36 red hits—we lose. Sixth time out 15 black hits — we lose. Because we've lost on the first 6 times, we now change to 2 chips on each number and come out with number 28 black winning. We lose. Second time out 14 red hits—

we lose. Third time out, 17 black hits—we lose. Fourth time out the double zero hits—we lose. Fifth time out, 19 in the red hits—we lose.

Because we have run through the second sequence 5 times, we now change to 3 chips on each number and run through this procedure 4 times. And coming out on the first spin, 34 red hits—we lose. Second time, 6 black hits—we lose. Third time, 33 black hits—we lose. Fourth time, 6 black hits—we lose. Because we have lost on the third sequence 4 times, we now change to 4 chips on each number and come out for 3 times.

Coming out on the first spin, 11 black hits—we win, paying 35 to 1 and giving us a total of $140. However, we have lost $12 on the other 3 numbers plus $128 for a total of $140. Net profit at this point is zero. Because we won, we now double the number of chips on each one so we have $32 going on the spin of the wheel. Number 34 red hits, giving us a loss. Now, because we lose, we would return to the top of chart 1 again, starting out betting $1 on each number and coming out with this procedure 6 times.

Let us take a minute to check to see how much money we have won or lost during the last few games. At the end of 38 games we have lost a total of $279. However, we have won a total of $315 giving us a net profit of $36.

We have played for approximately three-quarters of an hour and have made $36. We would now return to chart 1 and place one chip, representing $1, for the next 6 spins of the wheel. First spin, 18 red—we lose. Second spin, 35 black—we lose. Third spin, 11 black—we win.

			WON	LOST
(1)	$ 4.00	18R		1
(2)	$ 4.00	35B		1
(3)	$ 4.00	11B	Won $35.00	
			Lost 3.00	
			Profit $32.00	
(1)²	$ 8.00	7R	Won $70.00	
			Lost 6.00	
			Profit $64.00	
(1)⁴	$16.00	29B		1

We have now won $35. Because we have won, we will now place 2 chips on the 4 numbers for one roll. Number 7 red wins. Because we are playing number 7, we have won again making a total of $70, less $6 which we lost on the other 3 numbers plus $11 on previous spins, giving us a net profit of $88.

Because we have won, we now double the number of chips, again placing 4 on each of the 4 numbers. Number 29 black hits—we lose. Because we have lost, we now return to the top of the chart and bet one chip on each number. At this moment, adding the total amount of money spent to the total amount of money won, we show a profit of $80. Little wonder this method is called Wear Out The Dealer. It can go on and on for many hours.

The idea is to be satisfied with a set amount of money that you wish to make in proportion to the amount of money that you are playing for. If you should hit 3 consecutive wins in a row, having doubled the number of chips on each number, you make a large amount of money in a very short time. However, it is possible to play for the 20 consecutive spins of the wheel and lose your bankroll, without having experienced one win. I recommend that should you wish to play this particular method, do so playing 25¢ chips, for should you lose, the greatest amount you can lose is $50.

One of the greatest hazards in gambling today is that people increase their bets when they lose. They will invariably spend more time at the table when they are losing than when they are winning. This is a bad procedure. When you are losing, remember: decrease the amount of money you are betting so that when the cycle changes and you start to win you will have the opportunity of riding the cycle to the crest.

It's more difficult to manage money properly and hold on to the winnings than to win the money in the first place. A good gambler does not use the defeatist attitude. He sets forth his plan, he controls his money and he does not deviate under any circumstances.

Roulette.

TWO-TO-ONE-ODDS.

You will notice, in looking at your diagram on page 179 that the first, second and third 12 each pay 2 to 1. When applying my method at roulette, I normally play red, black, odd, even, high and low, which pay even money.

EXAMPLE:
If I bet $50 on red, black, odd, even, high or low and I win, I would win $50. In playing my method, if we were to play the first, second or third column, we would win twice the amount of money that we bet.

EXAMPLE:
Let us say we placed $50 on the second 12. This means that we are covering numbers from 13 to 24. If any of those numbers should hit on this particular spin, we would win $100 for our $50 investment. Compare this with winning even money playing any one of the 6 on the outside line.

Now, let us suppose that we had a bankroll of $3,000 and we were playing a sequence to make $150. By playing red, black, odd, even, high, or low, we would at the end of the sequence have made our $150. If we had been playing the first, second or third

12, we would at the end of the sequence have made $300. While our losses would have been exactly the same no matter which method we had been playing, we would have gained 2 to 1 on our wins. The same, of course, would apply if we were playing the first, second or third column. However, I would not recommend this procedure. The system will work, but it takes longer.

EXAMPLE:

Forgetting the greens on the wheel, if you were to bet in the second 12 you are covering 12 numbers while the house has 24. But if you were playing black you are covering 18 numbers while you have 18 red numbers against you. So I suggest that you play the outside line where even-given odds are employed, excluding the greens.

Adjacent numbers.

You will note on page 182 a table of adjacent numbers. These tables are usually put out by the casinos to assist players in betting roulette. It makes no difference where in the world you are playing; the table of adjacent numbers is the same on any American wheel but different on the European wheel.

Looking at the chart on page 182, let us take number 11. If 11 has hit on the wheel, the statistics state that the next number to hit on the wheel would be 6, 27, 13, 36, 30, 8, 23 or 10. This does not mean that one of these eight numbers will hit, but it helps minimize the guesswork to stick to statistics.

Looking on further down the page, at number 19, we see that 26, 0, 32, 15, 4, 21, 2 or 25 should hit. You will also notice throughout the table that some numbers are repeated in many cases. This does not specifically say that you are definitely going to win. The table is merely an aid.

American wheels, European wheels.

You will notice the difference between the American roulette wheel and the European roulette wheel. Let us take the American roulette wheel first. On the American wheel, we have a single zero (0) and a double zero (00), which gives the house the edge by approximately 5½%. If you have your money placed on any one of the 36 numbers, in the first second or third columns, the 1, 2 or 3, 12, red, black, odd, even, high or low, and one of the greens should appear on the wheel, you lose your money. Only if you are betting the single zero or the double zero and it hits, do you win. You are paid 35 to 1, the same as the numbers.

Now looking at the European wheel, you will notice there is only a single zero. Therefore, the house advantage is only about 3½%. If you were playing, high, low, odd, even, red or black and green should appear, instead of losing your money like you would on the American wheel, your money is placed behind a line called a prison and remains there for the next spin of the wheel. Let us suppose we had been playing black and green should appear. Our money is then placed behind the line on the black side of the table for the next spin. If the next spin should be any of the black numbers, our money is then placed back in action, giving you another chance to win. However, while your money is in prison, if the wheel should come up showing a red number, then you have lost.

The European wheel definitely gives an additional advantage to the player.

Playing on the craps table.

You will notice, looking at the layout of the craps table on page 202, that the field bet gives you the greatest number of numbers coming out on the roll of the dice. In other words, if you place a $10 bet on the field and numbers 2, 3, 4, 9, 10, 11 or 12 hit on the roll of the dice you win: $10 for your $10 bet on 3, 4, 9, 10, 11; $20 for your bet on 2; $30 for your bet on 12.

Many people feel that by playing the field their chances of winning are greatly increased, but take it from me, this is known as a sucker's bet. Numbers 6, 7 and 8, which are not included in the field, can be made 3 different ways on the dice while the field numbers can be made only 2 different ways; therefore, the house has the advantage of the extra percentage of a 6, 7, or 8 appearing. I have seen thousands of dollars won by playing the field. It boils down to one thing — hitting the table at the right moment.

The odds on a craps table, if you were playing the pass line or betting with the shooter, would be approximately 1¼% to 1½% against you. However, if you were to play the don't pass where you are playing against the shooter, the percentage against you is only ½%. Based on experience, I very seldom play on the pass line unless I play the hot and cold method at the same time.

Let me explain. If the house wishes to win from a certain person by putting in crooked dice, the only way that it can win is by putting in dice that would roll 2, 3 or 12; therefore if you were playing the pass line you would be experiencing many losses because of the crooked dice. However, if you were playing the don't pass line and the house should throw crooked dice into the game, then, because the dice thrower is losing, you are automatically winning.

Another method for the house to beat the player is if the shooter has come out for his point, say 6; the house could then put in dice that would roll a 7. Once again, if you are playing the don't pass line,

CRAP TABLE

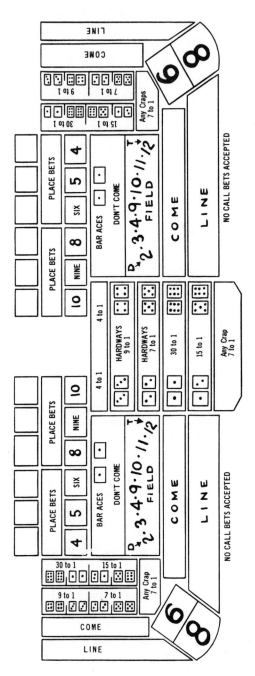

* D No. 2 on field pays DOUBLE
* T No. 12 on field pays TRIPLE

you would win; for any 7 thrown after the point has been established, the don't pass line wins.

When I play, I play the don't pass line, not because it gives me any better percentage but because it offers added protection should the house be manipulating the dice. I very seldom make any place bets or a back line bets. I usually lay odds whether I am playing on the pass line or the don't pass line. I never bet on the hardways or on the field. I place my specific amount of money on either the come or the don't come and I am satisfied with the small returns I make.

During my travels around the world visiting many casinos, I have seen many systems played. The 5, 10 and 15 system seems to be one of the most commonly played by people who do not really understand the full game of dice or craps but merely play the pass or don't pass line.

These people would play by betting $5, and if they win they would increase the bet to $10. If they should win with their $10 bet they would increase it to $15. They would continue to play at $15 until they lost, at which time they would revert back to betting $5 and continue to do so until they won, at which time they would increase it to $10 again. Never at any time would they bet more than $15, and should they experience a bad roll of the dice they would be betting a nominal sum of $5 each time.

This is a good method because it helps to protect the money you are carrying, and the important thing to remember is always protect what you have in your pocket.

When I am playing at the craps table I occasionally lay the odds on a 4 and a 10 if I am playing the don't pass; the odds are 2 to 1 that he will roll a 7 before a 4 or 10. I always lay odds if the point is 5 or 9, for the odds are 3 to 2 that he will roll a 7 before his point. If I am playing the pass line I place odds on all my bets. Whether you are playing a method or simply gambling for fun, to not place odds is a waste of time at the table.

I very seldom make place bets on the back of the line on numbers 4, 5, 6, 8, 9 and 10; however, occasionally I will place a bet on the come line on each roll of the dice.

One thing I would like to bring to your attention is that pay-offs differ from club to club. For instance, if you were playing in one casino and they paid off at 15 to 1, that means that you would receive $15 plus the $1 that you bet. However, in other casinos you would only be paid $14 plus the $1 that you initially bet if the pay-off was 15 for 1.

Blackjack.

The odds against the player in blackjack are extremely high. If there are 6 people playing at the tables and they played non-stop, the statistics governing the percentage against them could be determined. However, take one player away and put another player in his place and the odds change. The way this new player draws his cards will change the cards for the rest of the players at the table.

After many months of play at the roulette and craps table, I enjoyed playing blackjack. It was the only spot where, I felt, I had an opportunity to become part of the game. If I was dealt 2 cards totalling 12, 13, 14 or 15, I alone had the opportunity of drawing or standing.

I have played blackjack where I draw the cards as I see fit. However, I can play the game by standing pat with the 2 cards dealt and putting the onus on the dealer to draw and bust. It may take me longer to make the amount of money I have predetermined, and certainly playing this way gives the house a greater percentage. However, it's only a matter of time before I have completed my sequence and gained the amount of money that I wish to make.

It is very difficult to tell someone how to play blackjack properly. When I first started to play blackjack in the early 1960's it was because I was bored with playing roulette and craps. So it was natural to find a game which was not boring and had some entertainment value. In those days there was no such thing as basic strategy. If a player had a 14 and the dealer was showing a 4 you would draw to your 14 or try to get as close to 21 as possible. Today things have changed drastically.

A person who has never played blackjack before has a 16% to 20% chance of winning. If he plays basic strategy perfectly — knows when to draw, when to split, when to double down, and most importantly when to draw against which hand the dealer may have — he has only a 49½% chance of winning. The House has a 50½% chance.

If he is a card counter and an exceptionally good one he will only increase his chances maximum 3% for a total of 52½%.

If he is a money manager and using only basic strategy he has a 100% advantage.

It is extremely difficult to sit at a blackjack table, play the game perfectly using basic strategy, counting cards and managing your money.

However, with a little knowledge of the game and proper money management you can be a winner each time you sit down and play.

Rather than explain basic strategy you will find a card at the rear of the book on page 222 that you can cut out and put in your wallet. This card will assist you greatly to make the proper moves depending upon the dealer's up-card.

It is important to realize from the beginning that even though you may play basic strategy properly, there is no guarantee that you will win on the hand you play.

I have played in casinos all over the world and have found from time to time that even playing the proper way, and drawing on the proper hands I still lost. I have also played the reverse of basic strategy and won. However, I have won more times playing properly than playing improperly.

Blackjack is a tough game to beat at the best of times, although it is the most popular of all casino games because people relate to cards rather than craps or roulette.

One important point I would like to make, always split Aces and 8's for they are a dead man's hand.

The Winner's Edge Midas Method

The following pages contain the method that I have used while visiting gambling casinos all over the world.

It is not difficult to understand or apply. It does require concentration.

Because my method is slightly similar to the Labby Method, I have played a number of games using both methods. You can follow each one, seeing the advantage that mine has over the Labby Method.

The method that I use can be applied to such games as roulette, blackjack, craps, baccarat-chemin de fer, chuck-a-luck, under-seven-and-over-seven or any other game that employs even given odds. (If you were to bet $50, you would either win $50 or lose $50.) This method cannot be applied to a poker game (unless it is showdown) or where you bet a specific amount of money at one time and either win or lose.

My method requires you to carefully control the amount of money you bet. When you win, you increase the amount of your next bet; when you lose, you decrease the amount of your next bet.

The method works like this:

1. First, decide how much money you want to win. Let us say $50 for this example.

2. Divide the amount you wish to win ($50) into four smaller amounts of approximately 40% for the first amount and 20% for each of the last three amounts.

$20 $10 $10 $10

3. Now, your first bet is the amount of the first number in this sequence—in this case $20. If you win, you cross the $20 off and bet the

total of the first and last remaining numbers in the sequence:

if you win ... $2̶0̶ $10 $10 $1̶0̶

next bet = $10 $10 = $20

If, however, you lose on the first bet, you do not cross the $20 off the list—instead you add the amount to the end of the sequence. Your sequence would look like this after a loss:

if you lose ... $20 $10 $10 $10 $20

Your next bet would be only the first number in the sequence — again $20.

This process is repeated until all the numbers are crossed off the sequence. If you win, cross off the number and bet the total of the remaining first and last number in the sequence. If you lose, don't cross anything off—instead add the amount lost to the end of the sequence and bet only the first remaining number in the sequence.

EXAMPLE: Play to win $50.

Divide the $50 into four parts: $20 $10 $10 $10.

1st bet	$20	Always bet the first number in the sequence. YOU WIN—cross the $20 off your sequence. $2̶0̶ $10 $10 $10.
2nd bet	$20	Since you won last time, bet the total of the first and last remaining numbers in the sequence. YOU LOSE—add the $20 to the end of the sequence. $2̶0̶ $10 $10 $10 $20.
3rd bet	$10	Since you lost last time, take only the first number from the sequence for next bet. YOU WIN—cross off the $10. $2̶0̶ $1̶0̶ $10 $10 $20.
4th bet	$30	Since you won last time you bet the total of the first and last remaining number in the sequence. YOU WIN—cross off the $10 and $20. $2̶0̶ $1̶0̶ $1̶0̶ $10 $2̶0̶.
5th bet	$10	This is only remaining number in the sequence. YOU LOSE—add the $10 back to the end of the sequence. $2̶0̶ $1̶0̶ $1̶0̶ $10 $2̶0̶ $10.
6th bet	$10	Since you lost last time you take only the first remaining number from the sequence for your next bet. YOU WIN—cross the $10 off your sequence. $2̶0̶ $1̶0̶ $1̶0̶ $1̶0̶ $2̶0̶ $10.
7th bet	$10	This is the only remaining number in the sequence. YOU WIN—cross the $10 off your list. $2̶0̶ $1̶0̶ $1̶0̶ $1̶0̶ $2̶0̶ $1̶0̶.

All the numbers have been crossed off — you have won the $50 you wanted to win in seven tries. The number of bets necessary to make your money will change but the system will always work in the end.

Let us now follow through on the games using the Labby Method and my method. I don't know how many people are acquainted with the Labby method. It is one of the best, but there is one problem: if a player suffers a lot of losses he is apt to hit the table limit. Once having done this, he either has to break down his figures or stop playing — not because there is anything wrong with the system, but because he cannot bet any more than the limit. Many years ago the casinos placed a table limit to curb the progressive player — the kind who continues to increase his bets whether he is winning or losing.

With the Labby Method you add the first and last unit together, and if you lose you add this combined figure to the end, and again take the first and last figure for the next bet. If you win, you then cross off the first and last figure, and proceed to pick up the next combination of figures.

For example, let us say we wanted to make $30. We could use many combinations of figures, but let us take the figures 15 5 5 5. We would now take 15 and the number 5 at the end, which total $20, for our first bet. If we should lose, our figures would now look like this: 15 5 5 5 20.

Our next bet would be a combination of 15 and 20, so we are now betting $35. If we lose, our figures will look like this: 15 5 5 5 20 35. If we win, they would look like this: ~~15~~ 5 5 5 ~~20~~ and our next bet would be the first 5 and the last 5, to make $10.

As mentioned before, the danger with this method is that you can after many losses hit the table limit. The method which I use is similar, to a point. Let us again plan to make $30, using the same breakdown: 15 5 5 5. Instead of taking the first and last numbers, *I only take the first,* in this case, 15. If I lose, my figures now look like this: 15 5 5 5 15. Now because I have lost, I only take one figure, the first one: still 15. If I lose, my figures now look like this: 15 5 5 5 15 15. However, if I win then my figures look like this: ~~15~~ 5 5 5 15. Granted, I have not won as much as I would have with the Labby Method. But had I suffered 2 losses at the start, I would only be out of pocket $30 compared to $55 with the Labby. The point of my method is that it protects the money in your pocket, which is the most important thing. As you are losing, you decrease your bet; only when you are winning do you increase it. This is the philosophy of a good and successful gambler.

If I had won on my first bet, I would then take *the first and last number* to bet, and winning again I would then take the first and *last 2 numbers,* therefore crossing 3 if I win and adding the one figure if I should lose. After any loss, I only pick up one figure and continue until

I win. Then, when I win, take 2 and even 3 numbers. Never at any time do I take more than 3 numbers, no matter how many wins I have in a row.

The following are games run off using the Labby Method and the Midas Method, based on the charts on page 210 I have played the red, black, odd, even, high and low using the Labby Method below and the same games using the Midas Method (see page 209).

THE LABBY SYSTEM

RED

15 5 5 5 10
15 5 5 5

6 Spins — $60.00

BLACK

15 5 5 5 20 10 15 20 25 30 35 35 35 40 50 55
15 5 5 5

22 Spins — $60.00

ODD

15 5 5 5 20 10   15
15 5 5 5 20 5

12 Spins — $60.00

EVEN

15 5 5 5 10
15 5 5 5 20 35 50 40 45 45 55 35

18 Spins — $60.00

HIGH

15 5 5 5 10 15 20 25
15 5 5 5

10 Spins — $60.00

LOW

15 5 5 5 20
15 5 5 5 10 15 20 25 30 30 35 45 45 65 85 105
125 145 150 175 190

32 Spins — $60.00

THE MIDAS SYSTEM

RED
~~15~~ ~~5~~ ~~5~~ ~~5~~ ~~10~~
~~15~~ ~~5~~ ~~5~~ ~~5~~

                                        8 Spins — $60.00

BLACK
~~15~~ ~~5~~ ~~5~~ ~~5~~ ~~15~~ ~~20~~ ~~5~~ ~~5~~ ~~5~~ ~~5~~ ~~5~~ ~~10~~ ~~15~~ ~~30~~ ~~15~~ ~~35~~
~~15~~ ~~5~~ ~~5~~ ~~5~~ ~~5~~ ~~10~~ ~~15~~ ~~5~~ ~~5~~ ~~5~~ ~~5~~ ~~5~~ ~~5~~ ~~10~~ ~~20~~ ~~10~~ ~~25~~ ~~15~~ ~~30~~ ~~35~~
~~5~~ ~~40~~ ~~40~~

                                        56 Spins — $60.00

ODD
~~15~~ ~~5~~ ~~5~~ ~~5~~ ~~15~~ ~~20~~ ~~5~~ ~~15~~
~~15~~ ~~5~~ ~~5~~ ~~5~~ ~~15~~ ~~20~~ ~~5~~ ~~10~~ ~~15~~ ~~5~~ ~~20~~ ~~25~~ ~~10~~ ~~10~~ ~~10~~ ~~10~~ ~~10~~ ~~10~~ ~~20~~ ~~10~~
~~10~~

                                        42 Spins — $60.00

EVEN
~~15~~ ~~5~~ ~~5~~ ~~5~~ ~~10~~ ~~5~~ ~~5~~ ~~5~~ ~~10~~ ~~5~~ ~~10~~ ~~15~~ ~~20~~
~~15~~ ~~5~~ ~~5~~ ~~5~~ ~~15~~ ~~20~~ ~~5~~ ~~5~~ ~~5~~ ~~20~~ ~~15~~ ~~15~~ ~~20~~ ~~20~~ ~~20~~

                                        40 Spins — $60.00

HIGH
~~15~~ ~~5~~ ~~5~~ ~~5~~ ~~10~~ ~~5~~ ~~5~~ ~~5~~
~~15~~ ~~5~~ ~~5~~ ~~5~~ ~~10~~ ~~15~~ ~~10~~ ~~10~~

                                        19 Spins — $60.00

LOW
~~15~~ ~~5~~ ~~5~~ ~~5~~ ~~15~~
~~15~~ ~~5~~ ~~5~~ ~~5~~ ~~10~~ ~~5~~ ~~5~~ ~~5~~ ~~5~~ ~~10~~ ~~15~~ ~~5~~ ~~20~~ ~~5~~ ~~5~~ ~~5~~ ~~5~~ ~~5~~ ~~10~~ ~~5~~
~~15~~ ~~25~~ ~~20~~ ~~20~~ ~~20~~ ~~20~~ ~~25~~ ~~5~~ ~~5~~ ~~5~~ ~~5~~ ~~5~~ ~~10~~ ~~30~~ ~~25~~ ~~20~~ ~~20~~
~~30~~ ~~35~~ ~~40~~ ~~5~~ ~~10~~ ~~5~~ ~~40~~ ~~75~~ ~~45~~ ~~5~~ ~~5~~ ~~5~~ ~~5~~ ~~5~~ ~~5~~ ~~5~~ ~~5~~ ~~45~~ ~~40~~ ~~40~~
~~85~~ ~~45~~ ~~45~~ ~~5~~ ~~50~~ ~~40~~ ~~40~~

                                        108 Spins — $60.00

1st COLUMN

RED	BLK.	ODD	EVEN	HIGH	LOW	
W	L	L	W	W	L	
L	W	W	L	L	W	
W	L	L	W	L	W	
W	L	L	W	L	W	
W	L	W	L	L	W	
W^L	L	W	L	W	L	
W	L	W	L	W	L	
W^M	L	L	W	W	L	
L	W	W	L	W	L	
W	L	W	L	W^L	L	
L	W	L	W	L	W	
W	L	W^L	L	W	L	
L	W	L	W	L	W	
W	L	L	W	W	L	
W	L	W	L	W	L	
L	W	L	W	L	W	
W	L	W	L	L	W	
L	W	L	W^L	W	L	
L	W	L	W	W^M	L	
L	W	W	L	W	L	
L	W	L	W	W	L	
L	W^L	W	L	W	L	
L	W	W	L	W	L	
L	L	L	L	L	L	00•
L	W	L	W	W	L	
W	L	L	W	L	W	
W	L	L	W	L	W	
W	L	W	L	W	L	
W	L	W	L	L	W	
W	L	W	L	L	W	
W	L	L	W	L	W^L	
L	W	L	W	W	L	
W	L	L	W	W	L	
L	W	W	L	W	L	
W	L	W	L	W	L	
W	L	W	L	W	L	
L	W	W	L	L	W	
W	L	L	W	L	W	
W	L	L	W^M	W	L	
L	W	W	L	W	L	
L	W	W^M	L	W	L	
L	L	L	L	L	L	0•

2nd COLUMN

RED	BLK.	ODD	EVEN	HIGH	LOW	
L	W	W	L	W	L	
W	L	W	L	W	L	
W	L	L	W	L	W	
L	W	W	L	L	W	
L	W	L	W	W	L	
L	W	W	L	L	W	
W	L	W	L	L	W	
L	W	W	L	W	L	
L	W	L	W	L	W	
W	L	L	W	L	W	
L	W	L	W	W	L	
L	W	L	W	W	L	
L	W^M	W	L	W	L	
L	W	L	W	L	W	
L	W	W	L	L	W	
L	W	W	L	L	W	
W	L	W	L	L	W	
W	L	W	L	W	L	
W	L	W	L	W	L	
W	L	L	W	L	W	
W	L	W	L	W	L	
L	W	L	W	W	L	
W	L	L	W	L	W	
L	L	L	L	L	L	0•
L	L	L	L	L	L	00•
W	L	W	L	W	L	
L	W	L	W	L	W	
L	W	W	L	W	L	
W	L	W	L	L	W	
L	W	W	L	W	L	
W	L	L	W	L	W	
L	L	L	L	L	L	00•
W	L	L	W	W	L	
L	W	W	L	W	L	
L	W	L	W	W	L	
W	L	W	L	W	L	
W	L	W	L	W	L	
W	L	W	L	W	L	
L	W	W	L	W	L	
L	W	W	L	W	L	
L	W	L	W	L	W	
L	W	L	W	L	W	

NOTE (•Represents single and double zero winning which is the house percentage. Unless the single zero and double zero are played specifically all other bets lose.)

3rd COLUMN

RED	BLK.	ODD	EVEN	HIGH	LOW	
L	W	L	W	W	L	
L	W	W	L	L	L	
W	L	W	L	W	L	
W	L	W	L	L	W	
L	W	L	W	W	L	
W	L	W	L	W	L	
W	L	L	W	L	W	
L	W	L	W	L	W	
L	W	W	L	L	W	
L	W	W	L	L	W	
L	W	L	W	W	L	
L	W	W	W	W	L	
W	L	L	W	L	W	
W	L	W	L	L	W	
W	L	L	W	W	L	
W	L	L	W	L	W	
L	W	W	L	L	W	
W	L	L	W	L	W	
L	W	W	L	W	L	
L	W	L	W	W	L	
L	W	L	W	L	W	
W	L	W	L	L	W^M	
W	L	L	W	W	L	
W	L	L	W	W	L	
L	W	W	L	W	L	
W	L	L	W	L	W	
W	L	W	L	L	W	
L	W	W	L	W	L	
L	L	L	L	L	L	0°
L	W	L	W	W	L	
L	W	W	L	L	W	
L	W	L	W	L	W	
L	W	W	L	W	L	
W	L	L	W	L	W	
L	W	W	L	L	W	
L	W	W	L	L	W	
L	W	L	W	L	W	
L	W	L	W	L	W	
W	L	W	L	L	W	
W	L	W	L	W	L	
W	L	W	L	W	L	
W	L	W	L	W	L	
L	L	L	L	L	L	0°
W	L	L	W	W	L	
W	L	W	L	L	W	
L	W	W	L	W	L	

4th COLUMN

RED	BLK.	ODD	EVEN	HIGH	LOW	
W	L	L	W	W	L	
L	W	L	W	L	W	
L	L	L	L	L	L	0°
L	L	L	L	L	L	00°
L	W	W	L	L	W	
L	W	L	W	L	W	
W	L	L	W	W	L	
W	L	L	W	W	L	
L	L	L	L	L	L	00°
W	L	W	L	W	L	
L	W	W	L	W	L	
W	L	L	W	W	L	
L	W	L	W	L	W	
L	L	L	L	L	L	0°
L	W	W	L	W	L	
L	W	W	L	L	W	
L	W	W	L	W	L	
L	W	W	L	L	W	
W	L	W	L	L	W	
W	L	W	L	W	L	
W	L	W	L	L	W	
L	W	L	W	L	W	
L	W	W	L	W	L	
L	W	L	W	L	W	
W	L	L	W	L	W	
L	W	L	W	W	L	
W	L	W	L	L	W	
W	L	L	W	L	W	
W	L	L	W	W	L	
W	L	L	W	L	W	
W	L	L	W	L	W	
W	L	L	W	W	L	
L	W	L	W	L	W	
W	L	L	W	L	W	
L	W	L	W	W	L	
W	L	L	W	L	W	
L	W	L	W	W	L	
L	W	L	W	W	L	
L	L	L	L	L	L	00°
W	L	L	W	L	W	
L	W	L	W	L	W	
L	W	L	W	L	W	
L	W	W	L	W	L	
W	L	L	W	L	W	
L	W	W	L	L	W	
L	W	W	L	L	W	

LABBY

RED	WON	LOST
1st Seq.	20	
		10
	15	
	5	
2nd Seq.	20	
	10	
Total	70	10
Profit — $60.00		

BLACK	WON	LOST
1st Seq.		20
	35	
		10
		15
		20
		25
		30
		35
	40	
		35
	40	
		35
	40	
		40
		50
	60	
		55
	70	
	60	
	55	
2nd Seq.	20	
	10	
Total	430	370
Profit — $60.00		

ODD	WON	LOST
1st Seq.		20
	35	
		10
		15
	20	
	15	
	5	
2nd Seq.		20

2nd Seq.	WON	LOST
	20	
		10
		15
		20
		25
		30
	35	
		30
	35	
		35
		45
	55	
	50	
		45
		65

	WON	LOST
	35	
	10	
		5
	10	
Total	130	70
Profit — $60.00		

EVEN	WON	LOST
1st Seq.	20	
		10
	15	
	5	
2nd Seq.		20
		35
		50
	65	
		40
		45
	50	
		45
	50	
	45	
		55
	75	
		35
	70	
Total	395	335
Profit — $60.00		

HIGH	WON	LOST
1st Seq.	20	
		10
		15
		20
		25
	30	
	25	
	25	
2nd Seq.	20	
	10	
Total	130	70
Profit — $60.00		

LOW	WON	LOST
1st Seq.		20
	35	
	10	
	5	
		85
		105
		125
		145
	165	
		150
		175
	200	
	195	
		190
	255	
	210	
	105	
Total	1375	1315
Profit — $60.00		

MIDAS

RED	WON	LOST
1st Seq.	15	
		10
	5	
	15	
	5	
2nd Seq.	15	
	10	
	5	
Total	70	10

Profit — $60.00

BLACK	WON	LOST
1st Seq.		15
	15	
		20
		5
		5
		5
		5
		5
	5	
		10
	5	
		15
	5	
		30
		15
	15	
		35
	20	
	40	
	20	
	35	
	20	
	15	
2nd Seq.	15	
		10
	5	
		15
		5
		5
		5
		5
		5
	5	
		20
	15	
	40	
	10	
		25
		10
		10
		10
	10	
	25	
	35	
		10
		10
		10
	10	

Right-hand column (MIDAS running):

5	
	10
5	
	20
	10
10	
	25
	15
15	
20	
	30
5	
	35
	5
5	
10	
40	
	40
10	
60	
	40
10	
65	
30	
Total 505	445

Profit — $60.00

ODD	WON	LOST
1st Seq.		15
	15	
		20
		5
	5	
	10	
	25	
		15
	15	
	15	
2nd Seq.	15	15
		20
		5
	5	
		10
	5	
		15
		5
2nd Seq.	15	15
		20
		5
		5
		5
	5	
	10	
	10	
		20
		15
		15
	15	
	35	
	20	
		20

	WON	LOST
		20
	10	
	30	
		10
		10
	10	
	20	
Total	330	270
Profit — $60.00		

EVEN

	WON	LOST
1st Seq.	15	
		10
	5	
	15	
		5
		5
		5
	5	
		10
		5
	5	
		10
	5	
	15	
		15
	10	
		20
	5	
	35	

LOW

	WON	LOST
1st Seq.		15
	15	
	20	
	10	
2nd Seq.	15	
		10
		5
		5
		5
		5
	5	
		10
	5	
		15
		5
	5	
	15	
		20
		5
		5
		5
		5
		5
	5	
		10
		5
	5	
	10	
		15
	5	

	WON	LOST
	20	
		20
		20
	20	
	40	
Total	305	245
Profit — $60.00		

HIGH

	WON	LOST
1st Seq.	15	
		10
		5
		5
		5
	5	
	10	
	10	
	15	
2nd Seq.	15	
		10
	5	
		15
	5	
	20	
		10
		10
	10	
	20	
Total	130	70
Profit — $60.00		

	WON	LOST
	10	
		10
	5	
	15	
		30
	25	
	50	
		25
		20
		20
	20	
	40	
	45	
		30
	5	
		35
	5	
		40
		5
	5	
		10
		5
	5	
	30	
		40
	30	
		75
	35	
	115	
		45
		5

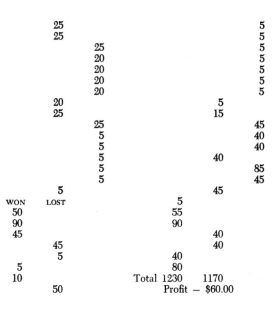

Looking at the chart on page 210 in Column One you will see a "L" and a "M." By playing the Labby Method and following the color red all the way down, the "L" stands for the Labby, and where I finished after having made the $60 I wanted to win. Further down in the red column you will see "M" which is where I made the $60 using the Midas Method. The same applies to all the other columns so that you will see how far I had to play with the Labby Method in comparison to the Midas Method.

Now going back to page 208, have your pencil and paper ready and start with the Labby Method, where you cross the first and the last if you should win, and if you lose you add the figure to the end and again pick up the first and the last figure for your next bet.

By referring to page 210 Column One and playing the red first, you will be able to check your figures against those on page 208, playing red.

The same applies for playing black, odd, even, high and low. Page 208 is a guide for you to check your figures to see if you have made any mistakes.

After you have played the Labby Method, refer to page 209 and the Midas Method and play the same games on page 210, Column One, under red.

Remembering to make the same amount of money, $60, by playing 2 $30 sequences and starting with the figures 15 5 5 5, you only take the first figure (15) for your first bet. We win, so we cross off the number 15 and our figures look like this: 15 5 5 5. Because we have won, we now take the first and last figures, which total 10, for our next bet. We lose, so now we add this figure, 10, to the end and our figures look like this: ~~15~~ 5 5 5 10. Because we lose again, we now take *only* the first figure, which is 5, for our next bet. We win, so we cross off the 5 and our figures look like this: ~~15~~ ~~5~~ 5 5 10. Because we win, we now take two numbers, the first and last, and our next bet is 15. We win. Our figures now look like this: ~~15~~ ~~5~~ ~~5~~ 5 ~~10~~. Because we win, we take the remaining figure, 5, for our next bet. We win, so we cross off the 5 and we have now made $30.

Because we planned to make $60, we now begin a new sequence of 15 5 5 5. Important: Only take the first figure to bet at the start of a new sequence, regardless of how many wins you had before.

Also, when you are crossing off your figures do so in this manner: ~~15~~ ~~5~~ ~~5~~ ~~5~~ ~~5~~ ~~5~~, and not in this manner: ~~15~~ ~~5~~ ~~5~~ ~~5~~ ~~5~~ ~~5~~. When you are playing at the tables, don't make it more difficult for your eye to pick up the remaining uncrossed numbers. This will increase the chance of an error. Keep things neat. You will find it easier to manage.

We have been working with the method in its simpler form—only using the first and last numbers no matter how many wins you may have. I have done this so as not to confuse you at the beginning. Picking up 3 numbers after you have had 2 wins in a row will be discussed later on.

Carry on playing the red, black, odd, even, high and low, using the chart on page 210. I have also kept a record on our wins and losses, which you will find on pages 212 through 215. Use this for checking.

You will notice that it has taken me more games to make the same amount of money with the Midas Method then in the Labby. However, the important factor is that the majority of my bets were lower than they were using the Labby Method, protecting my bankroll and undoubtedly staying further away from the table limit.

Now that you have had a chance to practice the Midas Method and correct any mistakes you may have made, we will carry on to the next stage—picking up 3 numbers after having had 2 wins.

Using the method where we start with any 3 numbers that total $30, such as 15 10 5, let us see the results by playing again the games of roulette on page 210.

Remember when we start a new sequence, only take the first number for the bet. If we win, take the first and last. For the third bet, if we have won the previous 2 take the first and last 2 numbers. If we have lost, then revert back to the first number.

We have left out red, for it was the same as before.

Black

~~15~~ ~~10~~ ~~5~~ ~~15~~ ~~25~~ ~~10~~ ~~10~~ ~~10~~ ~~10~~ ~~10~~ ~~15~~ ~~30~~ ~~55~~ ~~25~~ ~~35~~
~~15~~ ~~10~~ ~~5~~

Odd

~~15~~ ~~10~~ ~~5~~ ~~15~~ ~~25~~ ~~10~~
~~15~~ ~~10~~ ~~5~~ ~~15~~ ~~5~~ ~~5~~ ~~5~~ ~~10~~ ~~15~~ ~~5~~ ~~15~~

Even

~~15~~ ~~10~~ ~~5~~ ~~15~~
~~15~~ ~~10~~ ~~5~~ ~~15~~ ~~15~~ ~~15~~ ~~25~~ ~~10~~ ~~15~~ ~~50~~ ~~65~~ ~~60~~ ~~110~~ ~~50~~ ~~50~~ ~~50~~

High

~~15~~ ~~10~~ ~~5~~ ~~15~~ ~~15~~ ~~10~~ ~~10~~ ~~10~~
~~15~~ ~~10~~ ~~5~~

Low

~~15~~ ~~10~~ ~~5~~ ~~15~~
~~15~~ ~~10~~ ~~5~~ ~~15~~ ~~10~~ ~~10~~ ~~10~~ ~~10~~ ~~15~~ ~~30~~ ~~15~~ ~~40~~ ~~10~~ ~~10~~ ~~10~~ ~~10~~ ~~10~~ ~~20~~ ~~10~~ ~~35~~
~~30~~ ~~10~~ ~~10~~ ~~10~~ ~~10~~ ~~30~~ ~~10~~ ~~10~~ ~~10~~ ~~10~~ ~~10~~ ~~40~~ ~~30~~ ~~50~~ ~~30~~ ~~30~~ ~~20~~ ~~30~~ ~~50~~ ~~20~~
~~30~~ ~~70~~ ~~120~~

By checking back on page 208 you will see that we have made the same amount of money, but in fewer games. You will also note that only in a few cases were my bets higher in my method, played on page 209.

Important information.

At one time I used to play to make, say, $67. I thought that by placing my bets in odd numbers, the casinos would not realize what I was doing. I was wrong.

What happened was that I created a lot of curiosity. For here I was sitting at the table with $1,000 in front of me and betting $53 or $61. Little did I realize how foolish I looked. After this was brought to my attention, I realized my mistake. Since then, I only play for amounts that end in 5 or 10. I recommend you do the same.

Bankrolls.

If you have a $700 bankroll play one sequence for $10.
If you have a $1,000 bankroll play one sequence for $20.
If you have a $2,000 bankroll play one sequence for $35.

If you have a $3,000 bankroll play one sequence for $50.
If you have a $5,000 bankroll play one sequence for $100.

You can play for more but you never know what is going to happen on the next spin of the wheel, turn of the cards or roll of the dice. Rather than be greedy, be satisfied with a little. You can always play another sequence to make more.

Many times you will play and use only a portion of your bankroll. This is fine. You are carrying the additional money in case you hit a streak of losses.

REMEMBER, PLAY ONLY A SEQUENCE IN PROPORTION TO THE MONEY YOU HAVE WITH YOU AT THE TABLE. NOT WHAT YOUR COMPANION MAY BE HOLDING. NOT WHAT YOU HAVE IN YOUR ROOM OR IN THE CASHIER'S CAGE.

Now that you have had an opportunity to practise my method with a roulette wheel, cards and dice, let us go one step further.

You have probably found that many times you had a streak of losses ranging in bets of more than $20 each time. Let's say you have made a bet of $50, $70 or $90 and lost, so now you only pick up the first number of the sequence for *your next bet.* Here's what I would do. After I had 2 losses in a row, using the first figure of the sequence, if the figure is more than $20, I immediately cut it down to a $5 or $10 bet. If I lose, I then add the $5 or $10 to the end.

Example: Let's say after a few plays we have figures such as:

~~15~~ ~~5~~ ~~5~~ ~~5~~ ~~15~~ ~~15~~ ~~20~~ ~~5~~ ~~5~~ 35 ~~15~~ ~~15~~ 55 20 20 / 55 35 35
                                                                                1 2

You will notice that we had a bet of 35 + 20 because we had won before, so now we are betting 55. We lose. Picking up our first figure, which is now $35, we bet and lose. Again we bet $35 — we lose. Now, after having added the figures 35 twice to the end of the sequence, I would only bet $5 which I would add to the end so that now my figures would look like this:

~~15~~ ~~5~~ ~~5~~ ~~5~~ ~~15~~ ~~15~~ ~~20~~ ~~55~~ 35 ~~15~~ ~~15~~ 55 20 20 / 55 35 35 5
                                                                              1 2 add five
                                                                              to sequence

I would continue to bet only $5 as I was losing, therefore saving $30 on each roll and protecting my bankroll even more carefully.

After I had won, I would then pick up the numbers as before, for my next bets.

This may take longer, but you will be betting less should you hit a streak of losses. And, when you have completed your sequence, you will be ahead by the amount of the numbers you have added.

Now practice this with the chart on page 210 using Low, which was

the longest sequence we ran off, and see the money you save especially in the last few plays.

The Midas Method can be applied the same way at the craps table, no
matter whether you play the pass line or the don't pass line.

When I play the craps table I always carry extra money apart from
my Methods bankroll so that I can lay the odds. Whether I win or lose,
I keep that money separate. You can play the same method on the
field, however, I do not recommend this method of play.

The Method can be applied at the blackjack table, even though
the odds against you are much higher. It may take you a little longer
to complete a sequence, depending on how the cards fall.

Whether you are playing for fun or using any system, I recommend
that you position yourself at third base (next to the dealer's right).
This gives you a better chance, for you have the opportunity of
seeing the cards played before yours — which helps you make a decision to draw cards or to stand.

Helpful hints.

It is not necessary to finish any sequence at a particular table. As long
as you keep the figures, you can go to another table or casino, or play
again the following day to complete it.

DON'T BE GREEDY!

You will find that after playing the system in your home hour
upon hour, at some stage you run into a very long sequence. Naturally,
the longer you play red or black, odd or even, high or low on the
roulette, or pass and don't pass on the craps table, one choice will hit
more often than the other. In your home you will probably find that
after playing 23 to 31 sequences, you will hit a long run. However, if
you were in a casino you should only play 3 to 5 sequences at one
time, then take a rest. Not only does this keep you alert mentally, but
by hitting the table from time to time or going to another table, you
eliminate the long sequences which will develop after a steady period
of time.

I have found that rather than stick to one color all the time, if
you find you are losing more than winning switch back with the wheel
or table for a few spins, or switch against the wheel or table until you
pick it up again.

I have found that a lot of people get attached to red or black, odd
or even, and if at first they have a good winning streak they will

continue to play the same way all the time. REMEMBER THIS ... because black or red, odd or even, has been lucky a few times, this does not necessarily mean that it will always be lucky. To break the habit before it becomes difficult, learn to switch rather than play all the time on one color or on odd or even.

Your biggest problem will not be learning the application of the mathematics, but developing the guts to push the money out without becoming confused and nervous.

The Ten Commandments.

1. Determine beforehand the amount you wish to make.
2. Ask yourself, will my bankroll protect me?
3. Have your bankroll with you at the table.
4. Get your cash changed into $1, $5, $20 or $25 chips.
5. Do not drink when playing. (If necessary, drink only coffee or fruit juices.)
6. Do not spend more than fifteen to thirty minutes at any one table.
7. Set your pattern and stick to it.
8. Do not be greedy; have patience.
9. Do not frequent the same club too often.
10. Remember: You may sometimes win more on your luck—but half a cake is better than none at all.

REMEMBER — You are the one responsible for your own performance. Be satisfied with a little at each sitting. Don't let the fast money go to your head. IF ANYTHING, PLAY MORE CONSERVATIVELY.

Conclusion.

This book was not written to entice you to gamble, but rather to offer an informative way to help you win should you be frequenting the various casinos throughout the world.

Many people have suggested to me that because I have a system, I am going to put the gambling casinos out of business. This is absolutely incorrect. If anything I am going to increase the gambling casinos' business, because 92% of the people who read this book will lose. They will lose because of their own greed, or because of other elements of human nature. But if you play the various games with the method that I have set forth, and play as I have played, then there's no doubt in my mind that you will walk away victorious each time.

Read your Ten Commandments and study them, practice the various games at home until you are confident that regardless of what distractions are about you, you will not make any mathematical errors. Set out your plan and stick to it, for if you deviate or play out of proportion to the money you are carrying, you will undoubtedly find that you will be sitting at the table short of money to continue the next bet.

I strongly recommend that you play no longer than 15 to 20 minutes at any one table. Move about as frequently as possible. If you set out to make a specific amount of money, once having made it leave the table. You can always come back a few minutes later.

Don't be distracted by other people who may walk up and play hundreds of dollars on colors opposite to what you are playing and win. You must not lose confidence in what you are doing. You have before you a good strategic, mathematical method which will carry you over the rough spots and protect the money you are carrying in your pocket. Be satisfied with a small amount of winnings each time. And let us never forget that: "Chiefly the mould of a man's fortune is in his own hands."

BACON — OF FORTUNE.

BASIC STRATEGY (4 - Decks)
DEALER'S UP CARD

YOUR HAND	2	3	4	5	6	7	8	9	10	A
8 or Less	H	H	H	H	H	H	H	H	H	H
9	H	D	D	D	D	H	H	H	H	H
10	D	D	D	D	D	D	D	D	H	H
11	D	D	D	D	D	D	D	D	D	H
12	H	H	S	S	S	H	H	H	H	H
13	S	S	S	S	S	H	H	H	H	H
14	S	S	S	S	S	H	H	H	H	H
15	S	S	S	S	S	H	H	H	H	H
16	S	S	S	S	S	H	H	H	H	H
17 or Over	S	S	S	S	S	S	S	S	S	S
2,2	H	H	SP	SP	SP	SP	H	H	H	H
3,3	H	H	SP	SP	SP	SP	H	H	H	H
4,4	H	H	H	H	H	H	H	H	H	H
5,5	D	D	D	D	D	D	D	D	H	H
6,6	H	SP	SP	SP	SP	H	H	H	H	H
7,7	SP	SP	SP	SP	SP	SP	H	H	H	H
8,8	SP	SP	SP	SP	SP	SP	SP	SP	SP	SP
9,9	SP	SP	SP	SP	SP	S	SP	SP	S	S
10,10	S	S	S	S	S	S	S	S	S	S
A,A	SP	SP	SP	SP	SP	SP	SP	SP	SP	SP
A,2	H	H	H	D	D	H	H	H	H	H
A,3	H	H	H	D	D	H	H	H	H	H
A,4	H	H	D	D	D	H	H	H	H	H
A,5	H	H	D	D	D	H	H	H	H	H
A,6	H	D	D	D	D	H	H	H	H	H
A,7	S	D	D	D	D	S	S	H	H	H
A,8	S	S	S	S	S	S	S	S	S	S
A,9	S	S	S	S	S	S	S	S	S	S

H-Hit   S-Stand   SP-Split   D-Double